First World War
and Army of Occupation
War Diary
France, Belgium and Germany

51 DIVISION
153 Infantry Brigade
Princess Louise's (Argyll & Sutherland Highlanders)
1/6th Battalion
1 October 1918 - 31 March 1919

WO95/2882/2

The Naval & Military Press Ltd
www.nmarchive.com
Published in association with The National Archives

Published by

The Naval & Military Press Ltd

Unit 10 Ridgewood Industrial Park,

Uckfield, East Sussex,

TN22 5QE England

Tel: +44 (0) 1825 749494

www.naval-military-press.com

www.nmarchive.com

This diary has been reprinted in facsimile from the original. Any imperfections are inevitably reproduced and the quality may fall short of modern type and cartographic standards.

© **Crown Copyright**
Images reproduced by permission of The National Archives, London, England, 2015.

Contents

Document type	Place/Title	Date From	Date To
Heading	WO95/2882/2 6 Battalion Argyll & Sutherland Highlanders		
Heading	51st Division 153rd Infy Bde 1-6th Bn A & S. Hdrs Oct 1918-Mar 1919		
Heading	War Diary Of The 1/6th Bn A & S. H. For The Month Of October 1918		
War Diary	Sheet 57c 1/40000	01/10/1918	31/10/1918
Miscellaneous	5th Division	01/10/1918	01/10/1918
Miscellaneous	5th Division No. C.C.513/3/3	04/10/1918	04/10/1918
Miscellaneous	Table "A" Issued With 153rd Infantry Brigade Order No. 341	07/10/1918	07/10/1918
Miscellaneous	5th Argyll And Sutherland Highlanders		
Operation(al) Order(s)	153rd Infantry Brigade Order No. 348	14/10/1918	14/10/1918
Operation(al) Order(s)	153rd Infantry Brigade Order No. 351	18/10/1918	18/10/1918
Operation(al) Order(s)	153rd Infantry Brigade Order No. 352	18/10/1918	18/10/1918
Miscellaneous	H.Q. Mess	22/10/1918	22/10/1918
Operation(al) Order(s)	153rd Infantry Brigade Order No. 357	23/10/1918	23/10/1918
Map	Map To Accompany		
Miscellaneous	6th Argyll	25/10/1918	25/10/1918
Operation(al) Order(s)	153rd Infantry Brigade Order No. 359	25/10/1918	25/10/1918
Map	Map		
Miscellaneous	C Form Messages And Signals	26/10/1918	26/10/1918
Miscellaneous	18th Bn. Argyll & Sutherland Highrs		
Miscellaneous	Special Order By Major-General G.T.C. Carter-Campbell D.S.O. Commanding 51st (Highland) Division	26/10/1918	26/10/1918
Miscellaneous	Fighting Strength	30/10/1918	30/10/1918
Heading	War Diary Of The 1/6th Bn. A And S. H. For The Month Of November 18 Vol 43		
War Diary	Hordain Ref Map Sheet 51A S.W. 1/20,000	01/11/1918	30/11/1918
Miscellaneous	Parade To Be Held At Valenciennes at The Place Dame On Thursday November 7th 1918	07/11/1918	07/11/1918
Diagram etc	Grand Place, Valenciennes		
Miscellaneous	1/6th Battalion	11/11/1918	11/11/1918
Miscellaneous	Special Order From Brigadier-General W. Green D.S.O. Commdg 153rd Inf Bde To Lieutenant-Colonel S. Coats D.S.O. Commdg 1/6th A.& S.H.	14/11/1918	14/11/1918
Miscellaneous	Fighting Strength	30/11/1918	30/11/1918
Miscellaneous	Roll Of Officers		
Heading	War Diary Of The 1/6th Bn. Arg & Suthd. Highrs. For The Month Of December 18		
War Diary	Hordain France Sheet 51a S.W 1/20,000	01/12/1918	21/12/1918
War Diary	Neuville L'Escaut France Sheet 51a S.W. 1/20,000	22/12/1918	31/12/1918
Miscellaneous	A.B.C.D. Coys. H.Q.	21/12/1918	21/12/1918
Miscellaneous	Honours And Rewards		
Miscellaneous	Decorations Awarded Since The Battalion Joined	05/10/1918	05/10/1918
Miscellaneous	Roll Of Officers		
Miscellaneous	Fighting Strength	03/01/1919	03/01/1919
Heading	War Diary Of The 1/6th Bn. A & S. H. For The Month Of January-1918		

War Diary	Neuville L'Escaut France Sheet 51a S.W. 1/20000	01/01/1919	09/01/1919
War Diary	Belgium Bois D'Haine Sheet 6 Brussels Set "C" 1/100,000	10/01/1919	31/01/1919
Miscellaneous	Roll Of Officers	02/02/1919	02/02/1919
Miscellaneous	Fighting Strength	02/02/1919	02/02/1919
Heading	War Diary Of The 1/6th Bn. Arg & Suthd. Highrs For The Month Of February 19		
War Diary	Belgium Bois D'Haine Sheet 6 Brussels Set "C" 1/100,000	01/02/1919	28/02/1919
Miscellaneous	Roll Of Officers	01/03/1919	01/03/1919
Miscellaneous	Fighting Strength	28/02/1919	28/02/1919
Heading	War Diary 1/6th Bn. A & S. H. For The Month Of March 1919 Vol 47		
War Diary	Bois D'Haine Belgium Sheet 6 Brussels Set "C" 1/100,000	01/03/1919	14/03/1919
War Diary	Seneffe Belgium Sheet 6 Brussels Set "C" 1/100,000	15/03/1919	31/03/1919
Miscellaneous	Operation Order No 1/6th Bn Arg & Suthd Highrs	10/03/1919	10/03/1919
Miscellaneous	Roll Of Officers		
Miscellaneous	Fighting Strength	31/03/1919	31/03/1919
Miscellaneous	5 Division Troops		

WO95/2882/2

6 Battalion Argyll + Sutherland Highlanders.

51ST DIVISION
153RD INFY BDE

1-6TH BN A. & S. HDRS

OCT 1918-MAR 1919

FROM 5 DIV TROOPS

51ST DIVISION
153RD INFY BDE

WAR DIARY
or
INTELLIGENCE SUMMARY

(Erase heading not required.) 1/6th Bn. Argyll & Sutherland Highlanders (T)

Volume XLI

Army Form C. 2118.

Place	Date	Hour	Summary of Events and Information	Remarks and references to Appendices
SHEET 57C				
62.0.00	1-10-18		Battalion situated as follows:— Rear HQ & Transport Q.4.a.8.8. Adv HQ. "C" "D" Coys Q.14.D.5.5. "A" Coy P.12.D.5.2. "B" Coy Q.21.B.8.3. "A" "B" "C" "D" Coys working on road from Queens Cross to Gouzeaucourt, Q.30.a.9.8. Road in bad state owing to rain. Good progress made with drains & repairs. Work slow owing to traffic. Lt Col. S. Coats, D.S.O. proceeded on 7 days leave to Paris. Major R.H.B. Halonine assumed command of Bn. & Major H. McC. McNabra duties of 2nd in Command. The following officers still on detached duties:— Lt J.D. Ridley, 5th Div. O. Officer. Lt W. Muir att. C.R.E. Lt S.J. Martin 5th Div. Burial Officer. Lt J.E. Adam, 5th Div. Asst. Gas Officer, Lt C. Farquharson 5th Div. Water Officer. Lt J.A. Moon att. 27th Bde. R.F.A. 2/Lts. M.W. Ward & E.S. Brown att 1st Bn Norfolk Regt. Lt A. Shenker R.C. Course Rouen. Lt & QM. J. Scaife D.C.M. from 3rd Army Catering Course. Draft 2 O.R. joined from Base. CASUALTIES:— 3 O.R. missing.	A.A.
	2.10.18		Battalion situated & employed as above. 20 other ranks on leave. CASUALTIES:— Nil.	

WAR DIARY

OF THE

1/6TH BN. A. & S. H. FOR

THE MONTH OF

OCTOBER - 1918.

Army Form C. 2118.

WAR DIARY
or
INTELLIGENCE SUMMARY.

VOLUME XLI

(Erase heading not required.) 6TH BN. ARGYLL & SUTHERLAND HIGHLANDERS

Instructions regarding War Diaries and Intelligence Summaries are contained in F. S. Regs., Part II. and the Staff Manual respectively. Title pages will be prepared in manuscript.

Place	Date	Hour	Summary of Events and Information	Remarks and references to Appendices
SHEET 57c 1/20,000	2-10-18		BATTALION SITUATED & EMPLOYED AS FOR 1ST. 10 O.R. TO U.K. ON LEAVE. Lt J.J CRAWFORD REJOINED BN. FROM 521 FIELD COY R.E. Lt J.A. WOOD & 41 O.R. REJOINED BN. FROM 13TH & 27TH BDE. R.F.A. RECEIVED WARNING ORDER FROM "D" BTN DIV. AS FOLLOWS:- "6TH BATTN. ARGYLL & SUTHERLAND HIGHLANDERS TO BE PREPARED TO MOVE BY RAIL ON 3-10-18 TO REJOIN 51ST (H) DIVISION 1ST ARMY. ADV. H.Q. & A.B.C.D. COYS MOVED TO POSITIONS ROUND BN. H.Q. AT O.A.O. CASUALTIES:- NIL.	A.
	4-10-18		BATTALION RESTING & CLEANING FOR CEREMONIAL PARADE AT 3.30pm. BATTALION TO BE INSPECTED BY G.O.C. 5TH DIV. (J. PONSONBY, MAJOR GENERAL, COMDG.) 70 O.R. ON LEAVE TO U.K. CAPT. A.G. ALEXANDER M.O. REJOINED 14TH F.A. ON BN. LEAVING 5TH DIV. NEW M.O. (1ST LIEUT. JOHN WALTER MCELROY, M.R.C. U.S.A.) JOINED FOR DUTY FROM 14TH F.A. Lt S.J. MACKIN REJOINED BN. FOR DUTY. (5TH DIV. GRAVES REGISTRATION OFFICER) CASUALTIES:- NIL.	APP. 1
	5-10-18		BATTALION ON MOVE (SEE APP.) BN. DETRAINED AT ACQ. ABOUT 10pm. MARCHED TO VILLERS	APP. 2

Army Form C. 2118.

WAR DIARY
or
INTELLIGENCE SUMMARY.

(Erase heading not required.) 10TH BN ARGYLL & SUTHERLAND HIGHLANDERS

VOLUME XLI.

Place	Date	Hour	Summary of Events and Information	Remarks and references to Appendices
	5.10.18		AU BOIS, ARRIVING ABOUT 11AM. BATTALION BILLETED IN SUBURBAN CAMP. CAPTAIN W.R. BROWN CHAPLAIN LEFT BN. CASUALTIES:- NIL	
	6.10.18		BATTALION AS ABOVE. RECEIVED ORDERS FOR BATTN. TO MOVE DURING AFTERNOON TO WEST CAMP, ROCLINCOURT. LEFT VILLER AU BOIS AT 3PM. BATTALION WELCOMED (EN ROUTE) ON REJOINING 51ST (H) DIV. BY 17TH BN 9TH S.H., 14TH GORDON HRS., 16TH & 17TH BNS. ROYAL HIGHLANDERS & PLAYED INTO NEW CAMP BY PIPE BANDS OF THE TWO LAST NAMED BATT'NS. BATTN. NOW FORMS PART OF 1ST ARMY, 22ND CORPS, 51ST (H) DIV & 153RD INF BDE. CASUALTIES:- NIL	M.
	7.10.18		BATTALION SITUATED IN WEST CAMP, ROCLINCOURT. COYS. CLEANING & RESTING. BATTALION BEING REFORMED FROM PIONEERS TO FIGHTING TROOPS. ALL PIONEER TOOLS RETURNED TO ORDNANCE BASE & SURPLUS TRANSPORT TO ADVANCED H.T. DEPOT ABBEVILLE. WARNING ORDER RECEIVED RE 153RD INF BDE TO RELIEVE 11TH CANADIAN INF BDE IN THE DURANT AREA ON THE NIGHT OF 8TH & 9TH. CASUALTIES:- NIL	
	8.10.18		BATTALION SITUATED AS ABOVE. BATTALION (LESS TRANSPORT) LEFT ABOVE CAMP AT 4PM TO PROCEED TO NEW AREA. FORMED UP ON ARRAS - LENS ROAD & ENTRUSSED AT 7.0PM. DEBUSSED AT 1-5 AM 9.10.18 ON NOREUIL - DURANT RD. (C.12.a.11.) & MARCHED FROM THERE VIA DURANT TO SUNKEN ROAD AT D.I.8. CENTRAL RELIEVING 78TH CANADIAN BN. LT J.O. RAMSAY & LT W. MUIR POSTED TO 2ND BN. K.O.S.B. CASUALTIES:- NIL	APP. 3

A 5834 Wt. W 4973 M687 750,000 8/16 D. D. & L. Ltd. Forms/C.2118/13.

WAR DIARY or INTELLIGENCE SUMMARY

Army Form C. 2118.

VOLUME XLI

5th Bn A&S.H. & SUTHERLAND HIGHLANDERS

Place	Date	Hour	Summary of Events and Information	Remarks and references to Appendices
	9-10-18		BATTALION SITUATED AS ABOVE. COY & SPECIALISTS TRAINING. CLEANING UP ETC. CASUALTIES :- 1 O.R. DIED OF WOUNDS.	
	10-10-18		BATTALION MARCHED WITH 153RD BDE. TO AN AREA JUST WEST OF BOURLON WOOD. LEFT QUEANT AT 1-30pm ARRIVED AT 6-15pm. ROUTE, INCHY - MOEUVRES & BOURLON. 30 O.R. PROCEEDED ON LEAVE. CASUALTIES :- NIL.	
	11-10-18		BATTALION LEFT BOURLON WEST AT 2-15pm TO MARCH TO RAMILLIES. CANCELLED EN ROUTE & BATTN PUT UP FOR NIGHT 11th - 12th IN R.E. DUMP, 1 KM FROM CAMBRAI ON THE MAIN CAMBRAI - DOUAI ROAD. ARRIVED 11pm. MARCH VERY HEAVY OWING TO UNUSUAL TRAFFIC ON ROAD. 6 O.R. TO U.K. ON LEAVE. DIV. MOVING FORWARD TO RELIEVE 2nd C. DIV. CASUALTIES :- NIL. Lt. A. McFARLANE JOINED FOR DUTY	×
	12-10-18		BATTALION LEFT ABOVE BILLETS AT 6am AND MARCHED VIA CAMBRAI TO ESCAUDOEUVRES, ARRIVING AT 9-30am. RESTED IN FIELD OUTSIDE OF ESCAUDOEUVRES TILL 4pm. BATTALION PROCEEDED AT 4pm BY MARCH ROUTE TO THUN ST. MARTIN. 152ND & 154TH BDES IN LINE. 153RD BDE. IN RESERVE. 13 O.R. TO U.K. ON LEAVE. CASUALTIES :- NIL	×
	13-10-18		BATTALION STANDING BY READY TO MOVE AT A HOURS NOTICE IF REQUIRED. Lt. COL. S. COATS RETURNED FROM PARIS LEAVE & RESUMED COMMAND OF BN VICE MAJOR R.H.B. HALDANE. 6 O.R. TO U.K. ON LEAVE. CASUALTIES :- NIL	
	14-10-18		BATTALION SITUATED AS ABOVE. PREPARING TO MOVE INTO LINE TO RELIEVE 7TH BN SEAFORTH HRS. THE FRONT FROM LA MON BLANCHE TO 07.00.1 TO BE HELD BY "D" COY (CAPT R.M. AIRDRIE) ON RIGHT & "B" COY (CAPT. J.A. LATTA) ON LEFT. THE SUPPORT LINE TO BE HELD BY "C" COY. (CAPT J. GARDNER) & "A" COY. (CAPT. D. WATSON) ON RIGHT & LEFT RESPECTIVELY. BN H.Q.:- IWUY. BN TRANSPORT & DUMPED PERSONNEL THUN ST. MARTIN. SPECIAL PATROLS ORDERED TO KEEP R.	APP 4.3

WAR DIARY or INTELLIGENCE SUMMARY.

Army Form C. 2118.

VOLUME XLI

(Erase heading not required.) 6TH BN. ARGYLL & SUTHERLAND HIGHLANDERS

Place	Date	Hour	Summary of Events and Information	Remarks and references to Appendices
	14.10.18		CONSTANT LOOKOUT FOR SIGNS OF A GERMAN RETIRAL. SHELLING NORMAL. LT. N°MILLER & LT. J.R. STOCKDALE FROM PARIS. 2/LIEUT. E.S. BROWN REJOINED FROM 1ST NORFOLK BN. 2/LT. A. MCINTYRE JOINED FROM BASE. POSTED TO "C" COY. CASUALTIES:- NIL.	
	15.10.18		BATTALION SITUATED AS ABOVE. HEAVY SHELLING OF LEFT FRONT COY ("B") WITH 5"9.S. ENEMY QUIET THROUGHOUT NIGHT 14TH - 15TH. CASUALTIES:- 3 KILLED "B" OR WOUNDED	
	16.10.18.		BATTALION SITUATED AS ABOVE. USUAL PATROLS. SHELLING DURING DAY NIGHT INTERMITTENT. LT. J.H. STOCKDALE TO 153RD BDE. H.Q. AS SEN. Y.O. CASUALTIES:- 3 OR KILLED - 9 WOUNDED	
	17.10.18		BATTALION SITUATED AS ABOVE. OD LT. J. MACHIN FROM LEAVE. CASUALTIES:- 1 OR KILLED. 1 DOW. W. 1 OR WOUNDED	X
	18.10.18		BATTALION SITUATED AS ABOVE. REORGANIZATION OF BN FRONT ORDERED. NIGHT 18-19-10-18. "A" COY. TO TAKE OVER PORTION OF LINE FROM 7TH BN. A & S.H. FROM "D" COYS. RIGHT, O.14.8.66. TO APPROX. O.15.C.77. "D" COY. FROM MAISON BLANCHE TO O.14.8.66. "B" COY. SECTOR BETWEEN O.7.C.8.1. & MAISON BLANCHE. "C" COY. IN SUPPORT. ALSO COUNTER ATTACK COY. CASUALTIES:- CAPT. F. GREENLEES. MISSING.	APP 3
	19.10.18		BATTALION SITUATED AS ABOVE. SIGNS ON A RETIRAL ON DIV. FRONT. TIME 5PM. RIGHT FRONT COY ("D") CROSSING RIVER SELLE BY FOOTBRIDGE AT T.29.C.2.1. TO TAKE UP LINE ON T.29 CENTRAL TO T.23.A.6.3. IN TOUCH WITH 7TH A&S.H. ON RIGHT. PATROLS PUSHED FORWARD TO HIGH GROUND. LEFT FRONT	

A 5834 Wt. W4973/M687 750,000 8/16 D. D. & L. Ltd. Forms/C.2118/13.

WAR DIARY
or
INTELLIGENCE SUMMARY.

Army Form C. 2118.

VOLUME XLI.

(Erase heading not required.) 6TH Bn ARGYLL & SUTHERLAND HIGHLANDERS

Place	Date	Hour	Summary of Events and Information	Remarks and references to Appendices
	19-10-18	6.10 a.m.	Coy ("B") pushing forward same as "D" to take up line from T.23.a.6.3 to T.23.a.0.5. "B" Coy. in touch with 7th Bn. R.H. Counter attack Coy ("C") on railway from T.22.c.5.0. to T.28.o.2.4. Support Coy ("A") on road L.27.8.4.3 to T.34. o.8.3. Bridge over River Selle broken. Snipers very active. Road at T.27.c. heavily shelled. Capt. D. Watson 9.12 o.k. proceeded on leave to U.K. Capt. J.A. Kirkwood went forward & assumed command of "A" Coy. Bn. H.Q. moved from Iwuy at 10.30 am arrived at La Mon Blanche Fme. at midnight. Coys still pushing forward. Little shelling. Casualties:- 1 O.R. wounded.	A.J.
	20-10-18		51st Div. (H) ordered to continue advance, 116th Bn A&S.H in conjunction 7th Bn R.H. to push on from line of railway T.15.B - T.22.c.5.0 - Station T.34.a.9.9. to line of 3rd bound - T.15.B - East of Douchy - T.29. central. Bn. H.Q. moved to Fosse de Douchy arriving at 2.30 am. BDE. ordered river Selle to be crossed before dawn & high ground beyond captured. All bridges blown up. "B" & "D" Coys. crossed by improvised bridges. German snipers very active. Shelling normal. 2500 Civilians (including 120 invalids) found in Douchy. Very little resistance made by enemy during retirement. Bn. H.Q. moved forward at 11 pm to La Croix St-Marie, arriving 12.30 am 21-10-18. Casualties:- 4 O.R. killed & 16 wounded	

WAR DIARY
or
INTELLIGENCE SUMMARY.

Army Form C. 2118.

VOLUME XLI

(Erase heading not required.) 7th Bn. Argyll Sutherland Highlanders.

Place	Date	Hour	Summary of Events and Information	Remarks and references to Appendices
	21-10-18		Bn. ordered to withdraw to billets in Haulchin. 7th Bn. A & S.H. to be firmly established before with draw. Bn. H.Q. moved to Haulchin arriving at 6pm. Transport dumped personnel rejoined Bn. The Bn. (except "C" Coy) had just settled in billets when word was received that the Germans had counter-attacked at Thiant on our right. Bn. proceeded by outposts S.E. of Haulchin & holding itself in readiness to drive off any attack N.W. from Thiant 9.6 prevent enemy getting N.W. of Railway J.19.20. A heavy German barrage had been put down in front of 7th Bn A & S.H. but no infantry action of any kind developed. "C" Coy. withdrew to billets when Lieut. A. McIntyre wounded Casualties:- 1 OR killed & 1 OR wounded	N.J.
	22-10-18		Bn. billeted in Haulchin. Resting & cleaning up. 163rd Inf. Bde. ordered to relieve 154th Inf. Bde. in right sector. Bn. moved from Haulchin at 5.30pm & proceeded to reserve Bn billets in Fleury arriving there 7.25pm. 2/Lt S. Fowlds on special leave to U.K. Casualties:- Nil.	
	23-10-18		Battalion situated as above. Casualties:- Nil.	
	24-10-18		Bn. in reserve. Coys. moved forward at 7.30am in support of attacking Bde. (153) to area round Thiant. Bn. H.Q. moved at 8.20am to new H.Q. at Thiant (near boat factory) Bn. relieved 7th Bn R.H. in & Ibie. Casualties:- 1 OR Killed & 2 OR wounded	App 6

WAR DIARY or INTELLIGENCE SUMMARY

Army Form C. 2118.

VOLUME XLI

(Erase heading not required.) 6TH BN ARGYLL & SUTHERLAND HIGHLANDERS.

Place	Date	Hour	Summary of Events and Information	Remarks and references to Appendices
	25·10·18		BATTALION ORDERED TO ATTACK & CAPTURE BLUE DOTTED & GREEN LINES. B & C COYS. WITH A & D COYS IN SUPPORT ATTACKED AT 7AM & CAPTURED POSITIONS AS ORDERED. OPPOSITION FAIRLY STRONG. 2 GERMAN COUNTER ATTACKS WERE MET IN "NO MANS LAND" & REPULSED AT THE POINT OF THE BAYONET BY "C" (LIEUT W.D. BISSETT) & "D" (CAPT. K.M. ALLDROYCE) COYS. BN. H.Q. MOVED DURING EVENING FROM THIANT TO CHATEAU DES PRES. LT. GEN. SIR R.J. GODLEY. K.C.B. K.C.M.G. COMDG XXII CORPS COMPLIMENTED 51ST (H) DIV. ON THEIR CONTINUED SUCCESS & SPECIALLY WISHED HIS CONGRATULATIONS TO BE CONVEYED TO THE 6TH BN. A & S.H. (SEE APP.). BN. CAPTURED 79 UNWOUNDED PRISONERS. TWO BATTN. TANK GUNS. 10 M.G. & 1 T.M. GUN. CASUALTIES:- CAPT. J. GARDINER, LT. J.B. McGLASHAN, LT. W.D. BISSETT + LT. J.H. McGEE GASSED. LT. P. GRASSICK. KILLED 2 O.R. KILLED 2 O.R.M. 28 WOUNDED 30 O.R. GASSED + 1 MISSING.	APP. 7
	26·10·18		BATTALION RELIEVED BY 6TH BN. R.H. & WITHDREW TO POSITIONS AS FOLLOWS:- 2 COYS. IN BLUE LINE & 2 COYS. WEST OF BLUE LINE IN SLITS DUG ON 25·10·18 ON LINE J.21.B.8.2 TO J.16.0.6.2. BN. H.Q AT CHATEAU DES PRES. BATTALION RELIEVED NIGHT 26-27TH. 1 COY BY 1 COY 8TH BN SEAFORTH HIGHLANDERS. REMAINDER BY 7TH BN. A.& S.H. LT. A SKINNER FROM LEAVE. (LIEUT C. SHEARMAN/ATTON) DIED. J.M. PRINE & M.R. GALBRAITH. J. MONRO J. FENWICK. 2/LTS M.W. WARD.) CASUALTIES:- 2 O.R. WOUNDED. 1 O.R. GASSED	M.F.
	27·10·18		BATTALION WITHDREW TO BILLETS IN HAULCHIN. LT. G.J. NAIR ON LEAVE TO U.K. CASUALTIES:- NIL	
	28·10·18		BATTALION LEFT HAULCHIN AT 11AM TO PROCEED TO BILLETS IN LIEUT. ST. AMAND. & HAD JUST REACHED OUTSKIRTS OF HAULCHIN WHEN BATTN. RECEIVED ORDERS TO ABOUT TURN & PROCEED TO LINE TO FORM 154TH INF BDE. RESERVE. BN. H.Q CHATEAU DES PRES. C & D COYS IN VILLAGE OF MAING. A & D COYS IN FRONT LINE. SHELLING NORMAL. CASUALTIES:- NIL	

Army Form C. 2118.

WAR DIARY
or
INTELLIGENCE SUMMARY.

(Erase heading not required.) 6th Bn. A&SH. "Sutherland HIGHLANDERS.

Volume XLI.

Instructions regarding War Diaries and Intelligence Summaries are contained in F. S. Regs., Part II. and the Staff Manual respectively. Title pages will be prepared in manuscript.

Place	Date	Hour	Summary of Events and Information	Remarks and references to Appendices
	29-10-18		Bn. situated as for 28th. Enemy snipers active. "A" + "D" Coys. got 8x50 Heavily shelled about 6.30am. Infantry action developed. Attack repulsed. Enemy again attacked at 4.30pm. "A" was repulsed. A+D Coys heavily shelled. (A Coy Comdr. Lt. J.W. Mair. D'Coy Capt R.M. Allardyce). Bn. relieved by 4th Bns Canadian Regt. Marched to billets in Lieut. St Amand. Lieut. N Mair to U.K. on leave. Casualties:- Lt J.A. Wood wounded. 2 O.R. killed. 10 O.R. wounded. 1 O.R. missing.	A.
	30-10-18		Battalion moved to billets at Hordain. Casualties:- Nil.	
	31-10-18		Bn. situated as above. Coys. cleaning up, inspections, etc. Lt. A. Shearer + 2/Lt. E.S. Brown on leave to U.K. Major R.H.B. Haldane to U.K. on duty. Casualties:- Nil.	

App 1	Ref. maps to 51st (H) Div.
2	do.
3	Relief at 154th Bde.
4	Extension of front.
5	Relief.
6	Attack.
7	do.
8	Letters from Maj. Genl. Pomeroy.
9	Maps.
10	Roll of officers
11	Fighting Strength

Appx. Letters of congratulation.

[signature] Lieut. Col.
O/C 1/6th A&S.H.

War Diary

5th Division.

....

In forwarding the attached order from G.H.Q. with reference to the re-organisation of the Division, I wish to express to the Officers, Non-commissioned Officers, and Men of the

  1/6th A. & S. Highlanders,
  12th Battn. Gloucester Regiment,
  14th Battn. Royal Warwickshire Regiment, and
  15th Battn. Royal Warwickshire Regiment.

my sincere regret that the time has now come when the long association of these battalions with the Division is to be brought to an end.

The gallant deeds performed by all ranks, the unswerving devotion to duty, the loyalty and self sacrifice displayed by these battalions in the service of their King and Country, maintains the highest traditions of the famous Regiments to which they belong, the lustre of whose glorious records they have still further enhanced.

I cannot allow these Battalions to be broken up without expressing to all concerned my heartfelt thanks for the very splendid way in which they have fought, especially during the last two months. Their courage has evoked commendation from the higher command, and greatly redounds to the credit of the whole Division.

That the majority of those who have served me so well in the past may still continue under my command is my sincere and earnest hope.

           J. Ponsonby.

1st October 1918.
          Major-General,
         Commanding 5th Division.

5th Division No. C.C.513/3/3.   SECRET

O.C.,
1/6th Bn. Argyll & Sutherland Highrs.

Reference this office No. C.C.513/3/1 dated 2/10/18
(Addsd. 1/6th A.& S. Hrs., & 5th Div. "G" only.)

1. The 1/6th Argyll & Sutherland Highlanders will move to-morrow, 5th October, by rail from ROCQUIGNY. The Battalion will arrive at the Station at 11.30 hours, entrainment will commence at 12.00 hours, and the train will leave at 15.00 hours. An officer of the Divisional Staff will be at the Station to superintend entrainment.

2. The rail destination of the Battalion is MAROEUIL (LENS I..3) for ECURIE.

3. Transport will move by road under Battalion arrangements. Instructions as to route and staging will be issued later.

4. Rations for consumption on the 6th October will be taken. The rations for the personnel proceeding by train will be delivered at ROCQUIGNY Station by 11.30 hours to-morrow by the 5th Div.Train. O.C.,5th Div.Train will detail wagons to carry rations for the transport personnel and the animals proceeding by road. These will accompany the Battalion transport to their staging place, and after handing over rations, return to the Divisional Train.

5. All tentage held by the Battalion will be struck and handed over to 13th Infantry Brigade Hd. Qtrs., BUS, prior to entrainment.

6. Two lorries will report at the Headquarters of the Battalion at 08.00 hours to-morrow to move baggage &c. to the station.

C. Hawes.

Major,
D.A.Q.M.G.,5th Division.

4/10/18.

Copies to:- IV Corps "Q"
51st Division "Q"
R.T.O., ROCQUIGNY.
5th Divn. "G"
13th Infy. Brigade.
5th Div. Train.

FILE

SECRET. Copy No..... 3

TABLE "A" issued with 153rd. INFANTRY BRIGADE
ORDER NO. 341.
MOV. OF PERSONNEL BY LORRY.

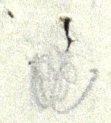

1. **EMBUSSING POINT.**

    ARRAS - LENS Road. Tail of column at Cross Roads A.28.a.6.3.

  DEBUSSING POINT.

    NOREUIL - QUEANT Road - C.12.a.1.1.

2.   Time of departure of column, 18.30 hours (Octr. 8th.)

3.   The Personnel of 153rd Brigade Group will form up on right of ARRAS - LENS Road, from Cross Roads, A.28.a.6.3. to about G.3.b.7.0., in two ranks, facing EAST, in the following order from the right :-

	Approximate Road space to be taken up.
153rd. Brigade H.Q.)	
153rd. T. M. Battery.)	100 yards.
7th. Black Watch.	300 yards.
6th. Black Watch.	300 yards.
6th. Arg. & Suth. Highrs.	300 yards.
400th. Field Coy. R.E.	100 yards.
1/2nd. (H) Field Ambulance.	100 yards.

4.   All personnel will be formed up by 18.10 hours.

5.   Captain McIntyre, M.C. and 2nd/Lieut. A.J.T. Wiseman, M.C. will act as Embussing Officers for Brigade.

6.   Each Unit will report its Embussing strength to Captain McIntyre at Brigade Headquarters by 15.30 hours.

7.   On arrival at Debussing point, Units will march to Billets as under :-

	Location.	Relieving.
153rd. Inf. Brigade H.Q.	D.7.a. central.	11th. Canadian Bde. H.Q.
153rd. T. M. Battery.	do	-
6th Black Watch.	V.26.a.1.6.	102nd. Canadian Battn.
7th Black Watch.	PRONVILLE	54th. Canadian Battn.
6th Arg. & Suth. Hrs.	D.1.b. Central	75th. Canadian Battn.
400th Field Coy. R.E.	V.25.d.0.0. (?)	Field Ambulance.
Mobile Vet. Section.	V.25.d.0.0.	do.
1/2nd (H) Field Ambulance.	To be notified by Staff Captain.	In their own Tents.
No. 3 Coy. (H) D. Train.	D.7.a.0.9.	Train Coy. 11th. Canadian Brigade.

  Staff Captain and Guides from advance parties will meet Units at Debussing Point.

8.   Lewis Guns and 12 Drums per Gun will be carried on the Lorries.

9.   Lieut. Colonel, F.R. TARLETON, D.S.O., 6th. Black Watch will command the convey.

10.   ACKNOWLEDGE.

                                                   Captain,

7th. October 1918.   Brigade Major, 153rd. Infantry Brigade.

Issued at 20.30 hours to all recipients of 153rd. Inf. Bde. Order 341.

152 B

6th Argyll and Sutherland Highlanders.

Report on operations from night 11th/12th October to the night of 28th/29th October, 1918.

On the night of the 11th/12th October, 1918 the Battalion under Command of Major R.H.B. Haldane was billeted in a Saw-Mill near TILLOY. These billets were left at 06.00 hours on the 12th and the march resumed. Route: Via CAMBRAI to ESCADOEUVRES where the Battalion bivouaced in a field. At 16.00 hours the Battalion resumed the march to THUN ST. MARTIN.

On 13th October the Battalion was standing by ready to move at an hour's notice.

Lieut. Col. S. Coats returned from PARIS and resumed Command of the Battalion vice Major R.H.B. Haldane.

On the night of 14th October preparations were made to move into the line to relieve 4th Seaforths. The right front from LA MON BLANCHE to O. 7. d. 9.1 was taken over by "D" Coy. (Capt. R.M. ALLARDYCE) on right and "B" Coy. (Capt. J.A. LATTA) on left. The Support line was taken over by "C" Coy. (Capt. J. GARDNER) and "A" Coy. (Capt. D. WATSON) on right and left respectively. Btn. H.Q. at IWUY. 2nd line transport and Dumped Personnel at THUN ST. MARTIN. Special Patrols were sent out and ordered to keep a constant look-out for signs of German retiral. Shelling normal.

From 14th to 17th October inclusive, Battalion was situated as above. Vigorous patrolling was carried out and contact maintained with the enemy to prevent his withdrawing unobserved.

On the 18th October the Battalion front was re-organised as follows :- "A" Coy. took over portion of front line from 7th Btn. A. & S. H. from "D" Coy's right (O. 14. b. 6.6.) to O. 15. c. 7.7. "D" Coy. from MAISON BLANCHE to O. 14. b. 6.6. "B" Coy. Sector between O. 7. c. 8.1. and MAISON BLANCHE. "C" Coy. in Support. Capt. T. Greenlees was visiting the Post of the left front Coy. about 08.00 hours on the 18th. He appears to have lost his way in the mist and walked into the enemy's lines.

On the 19th October about 17.00 hours scouts found LIEU ST. AMAND unoccupied. Patrols were pushed forward and in accordance with 153rd Inf. Bde. Order No. 354 the advance was commenced with 7th A. & S. H. on right and 7th Black Watch on the left. Btn. H.Q. moved to LA MAISON BLANCHE. The advance was carried out in three bounds.

First Bound. The NEUVILLE-SUR-L'ESCAUT - NOYELLES SUR-SELLE Road running through FRETE-au-POIRIER at I. 27. b. 3.5.

Second Bound. Line of Railway I. 28. d., b. and a - I. 22. c. - I. 21. b. - I. 15. d.

Third Bound. I. 15. b. - East of DOUCHY - I. 29. Cent.

No opposition was met with and during the night the advance continued to the above lines. Btn. H.Q. moved to FRETE-au-POIRIER.

At the bridge over river SELLE in DOUCHY a sniper was encountered.

"B" Coy. on the left. "D" Coy. on the right and "A" and "C" Coys. in Support.

At about 04.00 hours on the 20th., "B" and "D" Coys. crossed River SELLE by footbridge North of NOYELLES-SUR-SELLE and took up position E. of River. Enemy resistance was met with from the Wood at I. 17. Central and vicinity of house at I. 24. a. 93. Under a barrage at 10.45 hours the 7th Black Watch on our left advanced with us to a line about I. 18. a. 5.1 to I. 24. d. 6.2. Progress on the right was slower. "A" and "C" Coys. moved over River becoming Support and Counter-attack Coys. respectively. "B" and "D" Coys. advanced and reached line of the Canal in touch with 7th Black Watch on left. "A" and "C" Coys. relieved "B" and "D" in front line. "D" Coy. formed defensive flank along Railway and "B" withdrew to trenches at I. 18. c. Btn. H.Q. moved to CROIX ST. MARIE.

On evening of 21st. H.Q. and 3 Coys. proceeded to billets in HAULCHIN. Right front Coy. remaining until in touch with Canadians on left (B.M. 293 d/ 21/10/18). 7th A. & S. H. in touch on right. The Battalion (less "C" Coy.) had settled in HAULCHIN when an urgent message was received from Brigade that Germans had COUNTER-ATTACKED 154 INF. BRIGADE. This, however, proved to be INCORRECT. "C" Coy. withdrawn about 23.00 hours. Q.M. Stores and 2nd lines transport joined Battalion.

The morning of 22nd October, 1918 was spent in cleaning up. Battalion moved at 17.30 hours to FLEURY in Support to 6th and 7th Btns. Black Watch.

On the 23rd October, Battalion was in FLEURY cleaning and resting.

On the 24th the Battalion was held ready to move in support of attacking Battalions. At 05.00 hours. Coys. and Btn. H.Q. moved at 08.20, Btn. H.Q. to J. 31. d. 9.0. "B" and "C" E. of ESCAILLON River and "A" and "D" W. of River. Orders received to relieve 7th Black Watch. Btn. H.Q. moved to BOLT FACTORY, J. 15. c. 4.5., "B" Coy. J. 12. c. 10.3. to J. 18. b. 5.0. - J. 18. d. 6.1. "C" and "D" in Blue line, J. 11. d. 2.0. - J. 24. a. 5.4. "A" Coy. in Green line between J. 16. b. 2.7. and J. 22. a. 5.0.

On the 25th at 07.00 on the attack was carried out with "B" Coy. on left and "C" Coy. on right with the Blue dotted and Green lines as objectives. "A" and "D" Coys. in Support. At 08.20. the right Coy. gained the final objective but M.G. fire from LA FONTENELLE held up the left Coy. Btn. H.Q. moved from THIANT to CHATEAU DES PRES. The enemy counter-attacked on the afternoon but this was met with a Bayonet charge in which many of the enemy were killed and our line advanced about 500 yds. About 74 unwounded prisoners weren captured during these operations, 2 Anti-Tank guns, 10 Machine guns and 1 T.M.

On the 26th October, the Battalion was relieved by the 6th Royal Hdrs. and withdrew to positions as follows :- 2 Coys. ("A" and "D") in Blue line (MAING) and 2 Coys. ("B" and "C") E. of THIANT. At about 15.20, "D" Coy. was sent forward at the disposal of O.C. 6th Black Watch. The enemy had counter-attacked during the afternoon and this Coy. Commander helped to organise the defence. "A" Coy. was sent forward to the Green line as Support but under control of Btn. Commander.

On the 27th the Battalion left HAULCHIN was relieved and withdrew to billets at HAULCHIN.

On the 28th the Battalion left HAULCHIN and proceeded by route march to LIEU ST. AMAND. At the PYRAMID DE DENAIN, the Battalion was stopped and orders given to move to MAING in Support to 154th Brigade. Packs were dumped and the Battalion marched to THIANT where orders were issued to Coy.

Commanders. The 4 Coys. were accommodated in MAING and Btn. H.Q. at CHATEAU DES PRES. On the night of the 28th "A" and "D" Coys. relieved 4th Btn. Seaforth Hdrs. in the front line W. of MONT HUOY. 7th A. & S. H. were in Support with 1 Coy. on our right holding FAMARS.

On the 29th October at about 06.30 enemy attacked left Coy. but was driven off. At 15.45 a heavy barrage was put down by the enemy along our front lasting for about 20 to 30 minutes. The enemy, estimated about 250 strong, attacked our "A" and "D" Coys. debouching from MONT HOUY Wood but was successfully repulsed with Rifle, Lewis Gun, and Machine gun fire. MAING was heavily gas shelled during these attacks.

During the night of 28th/29th, extensive patrolling was done and a Post formed by the right Coy. on the edge of the Wood. The Post proved very useful during the counter-attacks. Battalion was relieved by 44th and 47th Canadian Battalions and marched to Billets in LIEU ST. AMAND.

S E C R E T.   Copy No. 3

153RD INFANTRY BRIGADE ORDER No. 348.

Reference Map :-
   Sheet 51.A. - 1/40.000.   14th October, 1918.

1.   The 153rd Infantry Brigade Group will relieve the 154th Infantry Brigade Group in the Left Subsector of Divisional Sector on 14th and night 14/15th October, as under :-

6th A. & S. Highlanders will relieve the 4th Sea.Hrs. on Right.
7th Black Watch will relieve 4th Gordon Hrs. on Left.
6th Black Watch will relieve 7th A. & S. Hrs. in Support.
153rd T.M.Battery will relieve 154th T.M.Battery in line.
"D" Coy. 51st M.G.Battn. will relieve "C" Coy. 51st M.G.Battn.

2.   Battalions will move up in following order :-

	Route.	Remarks.
6th Black Watch.	Track through N.34.c. & d. - N.34.b. - N.35.a. (to be reconnoitred)	Two rear Coys to reach Cross Roads N.35.b.0.9. at 17.30 hrs. 2 front Coys not to pass this point before 18.00 hrs.
6th A. & S.Hrs.	Cross Roads T.10.a. 6.2. - Rd.Junction T.5.c.4.9. - thro. old German Dump - along Railway to T.5.d.9.7. - Track to Railway N.36.d.0.2. (to be reconnoitred)	Leading platoon to arrive N.36.d.0.2. at 18.00 hrs. Transport cannot use this route but can proceed by Road to T.5.d.9.7. - thence along track.
7th Black Watch.	As for 6th Black Watch.	Leading platoon to reach Cross roads N.29.d.2.1. at 19.00 hrs.

3.   All other arrangements for relief and guides will be made direct between Commanding Officers concerned.

4.   Officers Commanding 153rd Trench Mortar Battery and "D" Company 51st M.G.Battalion will arrange their relief direct with Officers Commanding 154th Trench Mortar Battery and "C" Company 51st M.G.Battalion respectively.

5.   Officer Commanding 400th Field Coy. R.E. will detail :-
(a) the following sappers to be attached to Headquarters in the line, to assist in the construction of shelter and in locating enemy traps, if the Brigade advances.
   Brigade Headqrs. 1 N.C.O. and 2 Sappers.
   Battalion Headqrs. 3 Sappers each.

(b)   Necessary R.E. assistance for the improvement of the Left Battalion Headquarters at N.24.a.1.1.

The remainder of 400th Field Coy. R.E. will remain in its present location.

6.   Units will forward a map, shewing their dispositions, to reach Brigade Headquarters by 12 noon on 15th instant.

7.   Packs and Blankets will be dumped.

8/.

8. Transport and Q.M. Stores will remain in their present location.

9. Personnel and Instructors to be left out of action will remain at the Transport Lines.

10. The extra 50 rounds S.A.A. per man will be carried.

11. Brigade Headquarters will close at T.10.c.0.5. at 21.00 hours and open at N.36.c.4.2. on completion of relief, at which time command of Left Subsector will pass to B.G.C. 153rd Infantry Brigade.

12. Completion of relief will be wired to Brigade Headquarters by the following Code :-

6th Black Watch.	CARRY
7th Black Watch.	ON
6th A. & S. Hrs.	THE
153rd T.M.Battery.	GOOD
"D" Coy. M.G.Battn.	WORK.

13. ACKNOWLEDGE.

Captain,
Brigade Major 153rd Infantry Brigade.

ISSUED at 14.00 hours.
Copy No. 1 to 6th Black Watch.
      2   7th Black Watch.
      3   6th A. & S. Highlanders.
      4   153rd Trench Mortar Battery.
      5   "D" Coy. 51st M.G.Battalion.
      6   400th Field Coy. R.E.
      7   Brigade Signals.
      8   Staff Captain.
      9   S.T.O.
     10   War Diary.
     11   File.
     12   152nd Infantry Brigade.
     13   154th Infantry Brigade.
     14   5th Canadian Infantry Brigade.
     15   51st (Highland) Division. "G"
     16   51st (Highland) Division "A"
     17   51st (H) M.G.Battalion.
     18   51st Divisional Artillery.
     19   No. 3 Coy. H.D.Train.
     20   Brigade Supply Officer.
     21   Brigade Gas Officer.

SECRET.   Copy No. 3

153RD INFANTRY BRIGADE ORDER No. 351.

Reference Map:-
Sheet 51.A. S.W. - 1/20.000.   18th October, 1918.

1.   This office B.M. 158 of today is cancelled.

2.   The 6th A. & S. Highlanders will extend their front to the right tonight 18th/19th October and take over from 7th A. & S. Highlanders as far as a line MOULIN de PIERRE 0.15.c.3.0. - MON BLANCHE - AVESNES-le-SEC Road, 0.15.c.5.5.

   Reserve Company 6th A. & S. Highlanders will be used and 7th Black Watch will extend their Reserve Company to Right and occupy area at present held by Reserve Company 6th A. & S. Highlanders.

3.   Guides of 7th A. & S. Highlanders will be at Cross Roads 0.14.a.2.0. at 21.00 hours tonight to guide 6th A. & S. Highlanders into position.

4.   Completion of moves will be reported to this office by the Code Word "GOLD".

5.   ACKNOWLEDGE.

Captain,
Brigade Major 153rd Infantry Brigade.

ISSUED at 16.45 hrs.
Copy No. 1 to 6th Black Watch.
     2n   7th Black Watch.
     3   6th A. & S. Highlanders.
     4   153rd Trench Mortar Battery.
     5   "B" Coy. 51st M.G.Battn.
     6   154th Infantry Brigade.
     7   51st (Highland) Division "G"
     8   File.

APP 4.

SECRET.   Copy No... 3.

153RD INFANTRY BRIGADE ORDER NO. 352.

Reference Map :-
    Sheet 51.A. N.W. - 1/20,000.   18th October, 1918.

1.   The following moves will take place on night 19th/20th October :-

(a)   The 6th Black Watch will move into Assembly positions as under :-

    (i)   2 Companies 6th Black Watch will relieve all troops
            of 6th A. & S. Highlanders holding line along AVESNES-
            le-SEC - LA MON BLANCHE Fm. Road from Road Junction
            O.15.c.6.5. to Cross Roads O.8.c.8.2. (inclusive).

    (ii)   1 Company 6th Black Watch will move into Support in
            the vicinity of CHAPEL in O.14.c. and d.

    (iii)   1 Company 6th Black Watch will move to Reserve position
            in O.20.a. and b.

(b)   The 7th Black Watch will extend their front to the right, and
      will relieve the remainder of the 6th A. & S. Highlanders,
      holding the line between Cross Roads O.8.c.8.2.(exclusive)
      to present inter-Battalion Boundary (i.e. road running North
      through O.13.a. and O.7.c. and d.).

(c)   The 6th A. & S. Highlanders on relief will move into Brigade
      Reserve, as follows :-

    (i)   Battalion Headquarters and three companies will move
            to IWUY, into billets vacated by 6th Black Watch.

    (ii)   One Company will garrison the Brigade Reserve Line
            from O.25.a.5.0. to N.29.b.5.4.

2.   All moves of 6th Black Watch and 7th Black Watch will be complete by 22.00 hours on 19th October.

3.   The 6th Black Watch will not take over any posts N.E. of the AVESNES-LE-SEC - LA MON BLANCHE Fm. Road, which line is to be the forming up line for the attack outlined at Commanding Officers' conference at Brigade Headquarters this afternoon.

4.   All arrangements for relief to be made direct between Commanding Officers concerned.

5.)   Completion of moves will be notified to Brigade Headquarters by the Code Word "BRUGES".

6.   A C K N O W L E D G E.

                                              .... Captain,
                                        Brigade Major 153rd Infantry Brigade.
ISSUED at 23.00 hours.
Copy No. 1 to 6th Black Watch.
        2   7th Black Watch.
        3   6th A. & S. Highlanders.
        4   153rd Trench Mortar Battery.
        5   "D" Coy. 51st M.G.Battn.
        6   400th Field Coy. R.E.
        7   Brigade Signals.
        8   Staff Captain.
        9   War Diary.
       10   File.
       11   152nd Infantry Brigade.
       12   154th Infantry Brigade.
       13   4th Can. Infantry Brigade.
       14   51st (Highland) Division. "G"
       15   256th Brigade R.F.A.
       16   51st Divisional Artillery

H.Q. Mess.   War Diary.

I wish to express to all ranks my appreciation of the splendid work done by the Battalion during the last eight days.

Rushed into it when only partially organised as Infantry, you have already established a name for yourselves and I look forward with the utmost confidence to the future of the Battalion and that all ranks will do their utmost to assist in bringing the War to a speedy termination.

22nd October, 1918.

(Sgd) S. Coats, ~~DSO~~., Lt.Col.
Commanding 1/6th A. & S. H.

SECRET.   Copy No.... 3

153RD INFANTRY BRIGADE ORDER NO. 357.

Reference Maps:-
   Sheet 51.A. N.W. - 1/20,000.   23rd October, 1918.
   Sheet 51.A. N.E. - 1/20,000.
   MAING Special Sheet- 1/20,000.

1.   The XXII Corps in conjunction with the Third Army is to renew the attack tomorrow with a view to securing the high ground N.E. of the ECAILLON River.
        The 4th Division is attacking in the Right Sector of the XXII Corps with an objective running from L'EPINE in Q.2.b. through K.31.a. to J.30.d.7.7. They are to be prepared to capture the village of QUERENAING by a secondary deliberate operation either tomorrow or on the following day.

2.   The 51st Division is to attack in the Left Sector of the XXII Corps with objectives as shewn on the attached sketch.

3.   The 153rd Infantry Brigade will carry out the attack and will secure and consolidate the third objective (BROWN LINE) shewn on the attached map as the main line of resistance with outposts pushed in advance.

4.   All objectives, Boundaries, and forming-up positions are shewn on the attached map.

5.   The attack will be carried out on a two Battalion front, 6th Black Watch on Right, and 7th Black Watch on Left. Troops will be allotted to objectives as under :-

	6th Black Watch.	7th Black Watch.
To GREEN LINE.	Equivalent of 1 Company.	Equivalent of 1 Company.
To BLUE LINE.	Equivalent of 2 Companies.	Equivalent of 1 Company.
To BROWN and BROWN DOTTED LINES.	Equivalent of 1 Company.	Equivalent of 2 Companies.

        Each objective will be consolidated when captured.
        When the BLUE LINE is captured and consolidated, it will become the Main Line of Resistance and troops which capture the GREEN LINE will become mobile Reserve to Battalion Commanders and be moved forward in close support of BLUE LINE.
        On capture of BROWN and BROWN DOTTED LINES, Battalions will push forward patrols to endeavour to establish the line of Railway in K.14. - K.13. - K.7 and K.1.
        The 7th Black Watch will be responsible for clearing CANAL DE L'ESCAUT.
        A Battalion of the Hampshire Regiment will attack on the Right of 6th Black Watch, and a Battalion of the 12th Canadian Infantry Brigade will be on the Left of 7th Black Watch.

6.   ARTILLERY.
   (a) The attack will be carried out under an artillery barrage, which will fall on line of River ECAILLON (excepting opposite THIANT where it will fall on Houses East of the River) at ZERO, at which time troops will advance from assembly positions. The barrage will lift at the rate of 100 yards in 4 minutes.
        There will be a pause of 70 minutes on the GREEN LINE and 10 minutes on the BLUE LINE.

                                                        (b)/.

- 2 -

6. (b) On the DOTTED BROWN LINE being reached, a protective barrage will be put down 200 yards beyond for 30 minutes when Artillery fire will cease.
Should further Artillery fire be required, the S.O.S. Signal will be put up and Artillery will open for 15 minutes on the protective barrage line.
Should further artillery fire be required, S.O.S. Signal will be repeated.

(c) A Mobile section of 18-pdrs will be attached to each Front Battalion. Any direct artillery support required will be rendered by these mobile sections.
One Section R.F.A. will also be detailed to North of CANAL and will support the advance from J.5. by direct observation.

(d) Heavy Artillery will fire, with delayed action fuses, on different objectives, in order to help in rapid consolidation.
Barrage Map attached.

7. MACHINE GUNS.
(a) The attack will be covered by a machine gun Barrage, under arrangements to be made by Officer Commanding 51st M.G. Battalion.

(b) One Section of "A" Coy. 51st M.G. Battalion will be at the disposal of each of Officer Commanding 6th and 7th Black Watch for the operation.
Officer in charge of these sections will report to the Battalion Headquarters to which they will be attached at 20.00 hours today for instructions.

(c) Officer Commanding "A" Coy. 51st M.G. Battalion will be prepared to move his remaining 2 Sections forward to take up a position in vicinity of BLUE LINE, when the BROWN LINE is captured.

8. TRENCH MORTARS.
One Trench Mortar is allotted to 6th Black Watch and 1 Trench Mortar and the German Mortar to 7th Black Watch for the operation.
Officers in charge of the Trench Mortars will report to the Officer Commanding the Battalion to which they will be attached at 20.00 hours today for instructions.
Remaining 6 Trench Mortars will be in Reserve.

9. R.E.
(a) 3 Sappers of 401st Field Coy. R.E. will be attached to each Battalion and Brigade Headquarters to deal with any land mines or enemy traps which may be located.

(b) Bridges are being constructed to enable troops to cross the River ECAILLON. Allotment and instruction re these bridges have been issued under B.M. 330 of today.
These bridges will be carried by loading waves and once the Infantry are across the River, the R.E. will re-erect and secure the bridges where required.

(c) R.E. will erect two bridges, capable of taking Artillery, over the River at THIANT, as soon as possible after the attack commences, one on Main Road, and one South of the village.

10. ASSEMBLY.
Troops will be formed up with bridges in assembly positions, on the MONCHAUX - THIANT Road West of River ECAILLON by 02.00 hours October 24th. This will be notified to Brigade Headquarters by priority wire "O K".

11/.

11.   8th Argyll and Sutherland Highlanders will be prepared to move at ZERO plus one hour. On the BLUE LINE being captured the Battalion will move forward and garrison the GREEN LINE with 2 Companies. The Remaining two companies will be West of ECAILLON RIVER. Battalion Headquarters will be at J.31.d.8.6.
Order to move will be issued by Brigade Headquarters.

12.   LIAISON.
(a) Battalions will arrange to establish liaison at the following points during the advance :-

(i) Between 6th Black Watch and 7th Black Watch.
On GREEN LINE.
Cross Roads J.24.a.2/6. BLUE LINE.
Chateau J.18.a.8.2.
Cross Roads K.13.d.0.9.

(ii) Between 6th Black Watch and Hampshire Regt (11th I.Bde.)
Fork Roads MONCHAUX.
J.34.a.4.9.
Cross Roads J.30.d.8.6.
Cross Roads K.25.c.3.4.

(b) An Officer of 153rd Infantry Brigade will be attached to 11th Infantry Brigade Headquarters during the operation. He will report at 11th Infantry Brigade Headquarters at 02.00 hours 24th October.

13.   COMMUNICATION.

(a) Communication will be established between Brigade Headquarters and Battalions by :-
Wire.
Visual.
Wireless.
Mounted Orderly.
Pigeons.
Orderlies.
Contact Plane.

(b) A Brigade O.P. will be established at RUBBER FACTORY, J.15.b.5.5., and will be in communication by wire to Headquarters 7th Black Watch.

(c) Mounted orderlies are attached to Battalions and Brigade Report Centre for this operation.

(d) RED Ground Flares for communication with aeroplane will be carried, and lighted when called for by aeroplane. Special men in each platoon will be detailed for this purpose.

(e) A contact plane will fly over area of attack on 24th October.
Flares will be called for at :-
Zero plus $3\frac{1}{2}$ hours, Zero plus $5\frac{1}{2}$ hours, and Zero plus $7\frac{1}{2}$ hours.

(f) Brigade Report Centre is established at CHLLE LOUVIERE J.20.d.1.1.

14.   HEADQUARTERS.
Brigade Headquarters will be at NOYELLES-SUR-SELLE I.34.d.6.6.
6th Black Watch.   J.31.d.8.6.
7th Black Watch.   BOLT FACTORY, J.15.c.5.3.
8th A. & S. Highrs.   FLEURY.

12th/

- 4 -

14. (Continued).

        12th Can. Inf. Brigade.   ROUVIGNIES.
        Hampshire Regt.(11thInf.Bde.) P.7.d.5.3.

On the capture of the BROWN LINE the following moves will take place :-

Brigade Headquarters to BOLT FACTORY J.15.c.5.3.
6th Black Watch   ) along THIANT - MAING Road.
7th Black Watch   )
6th A. & S. Hrs.   to J.31.d.8.6.

15. REPORTS.
Early information is of utmost importance, and, in addition to reports, when the situation demands them, reports will be rendered at every clock hour after Zero.
Reports are required regarding :-
    (a) Progress of attack.
    (b) Action of enemy.
    (c) Enemy movement.
    (d) Enemy strength.
    (e) Disposition of enemy.
    (f) Any mines laid or destruction done by enemy, to delay our advance.

16. PRISONERS OF WAR.
Prisoners of War will be sent to Brigade Headquarters at NOYELLES-SUR-SELLE, I.34.d.6.6.

17. MEDICAL ARRANGEMENTS. will be notified later.

18. SYNCHRONISATION.
A synchronised watch will be sent to all concerned at 20.00 hours today, 23rd October.

19. ZERO HOUR.
Zero hour will be at 04.00 hours, October 24th.

20. ACKNOWLEDGE.

                                              Captain,
                        Brigade Major 153rd Infantry Brigade.

ISSUED at 18.30 hours.
Copy No. 1 to 8th Black Watch.
      2   7th Black Watch.
      3   6th A. & S. Highlanders.
      4   153rd Trench Mortar Battery.
      5   "A" Coy. 51st M.G.Battalion.
      6   401st Field Coy. R.E.
      7   Brigade Signals.
      8   Staff Captain.
      9   War Diary.
     10   File.
     11   152nd Infantry Brigade.
     12   154th Infantry Brigade.
     13   11th Infantry Brigade.
     14   12th Canadian Infantry Brigade.
     15   51st (Highland) Division "G".
     17   51st Divisional Artillery.
     18   51st M.G.Battalion.
     19   O.C. Corps Cyclist Coy.
     20   Right Group Artillery.
     21   34th Brigade R.G.A.
     22   Brigade Gas Officer.

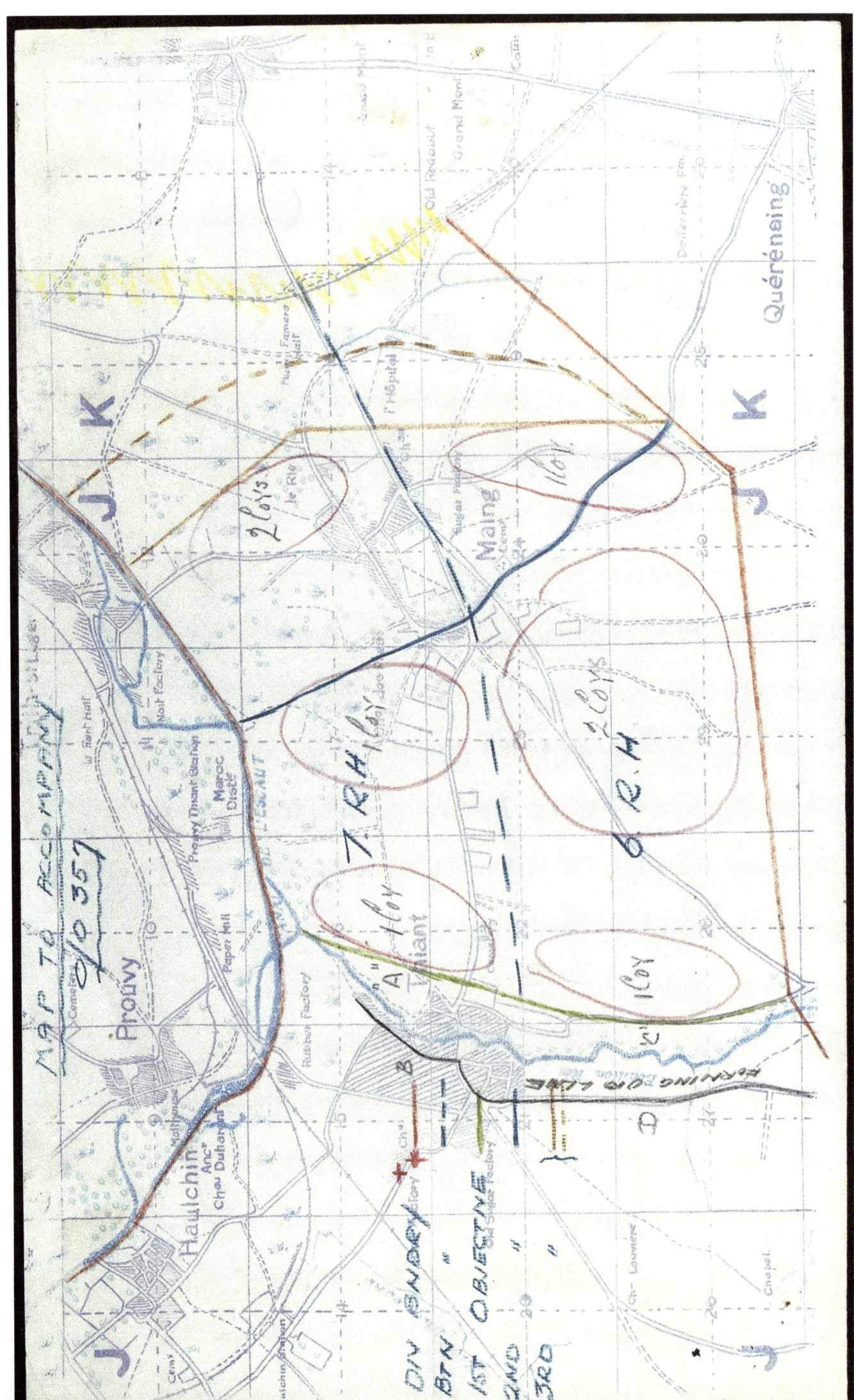

Well done 6th Argyll & Sutherlands
Highrs

W. Green
Brig Genl.
Comdg. 183 Infy. Bde.

25.10.18.

2.

S E C R E T.   Copy No...3...

153RD INFANTRY BRIGADE ORDER NO. 359.

Reference Maps:-
    Sheet 51.A. N.W. - 1/20,000.
    Sheet 51.A. N.E. - 1/20,000.
    MAING Special Sheet - 1/20,000.   25th October, 1918.

1.   The 4th and 51st Divisions are to attack today, 25th October to capture an objective which includes the village of QUERENAING, CAUMONT Fm., LA BATTERAVE Fm. ROUGE MONT and thence to K.7.c.5.3.

2.   The dividing line between Divisions runs from J.30.d.7.7. to crossing over railway at K.20.d.8.1., to cross roads K.21.d.3.4., to K.10.c.5.8. and thence N.E. along road.

3.   The attack on the 51st Division front will be carried out by the 152nd Infantry Brigade on the right and the 153rd Infantry Brigade on the left.

4.   Boundaries, Objectives, and Forming-up Line are shown on attached map.
    No troops to be East of BLACK LINE after ZERO minus one hour.

5.   The attack on the 153rd Infantry Brigade front will be carried out on a two company front.
    The 6th A & S. Highlanders will attack and capture the BLUE DOTTED and GREEN LINES, and should the enemy be found to be withdrawing, will push forward and endeavour to establish themselves on RED DOTTED LINE.
    Each objective will be consolidated when captured.
    Should the DOTTED RED LINE be reached, it will be held as an outpost line, with Support Line on reverse slope of hill.
    The 6th Seaforth Highlanders will attack on the Right of 6th A. & S. Highlanders, and a Battalion of the 12th Canadian Infantry Brigade will be on the Left.

6.   On GREEN LINE being reached, should Infantry be unable to keep touch with the enemy, touch will be gained by Cavalry and Cyclists.

7. **ARTILLERY.**
  (a)   Attack will be carried out under an Artillery Barrage, which will fall on a line 200 yards East of BLACK LINE, for 15 minutes, after which time it will commence to lift, and Infantry will advance.

  (b)   One Mobile section of 4.5" Hows. will be attached to Officer Commanding 6th A. & S. Highlanders for this operation.

  (c)   On the GREEN LINE being reached, a protective barrage will be put down 200 yards beyond for 30 minutes when Artillery fire will cease.
    Should further Artillery fire be required, the S.O.S. Signal will be put up and Artillery will open for 15 minutes on the protective barrage line.
    Should further artillery fire be required, S.O.S. Signal will be repeated.

8. **MACHINE GUNS.**
  (a)   4 Machine Guns of "A" Company 51st M.G. Battalion will be placed at the disposal of Officer Commanding 6th A & S. Highlanders for the initial attack.

(b)/.

8. (Continued).

  (b) In event of a successful exploitation, moves of Machine Guns will be as follows :-

  (i)   4 Guns at disposal of 6th A & S. Highlanders will move forward with advancing troops.

  (ii) 4 Guns will be moved to vicinity of RAILWAY.

  (iii) 4 Guns to BLUE DOTTED LINE.

  (iv) 4 Guns will be held in reserve on BLUE LINE.

9. TRENCH MORTARS.
   2 Trench Mortars and one German Trench Mortar will be at disposal of Officer Commanding 6th A & S Highlanders for the operation.

10. 6th Black Watch will be prepared, in event of successful exploitation, to occupy BLUE and GREEN LINES as vacated by 6th A & S Highlanders.
    Order to move will be issued by Brigade Headquarters.

11. LIAISON.
    The Officer Commanding 6th A & S Highlanders will arrange to establish liaison with 6th Seaforth Highlanders at Junction of Railway and Road at   K.13.b.8.3.

12. COMMUNICATION.

  (a) Communication will be established between Brigade Headquarters and Battalions by :-
      Wire.
      Visual.
      Wireless.
      Mounted Orderly.
      Pigeons.
      Orderlies.
      Contact Plane.

  (b) Mounted Orderlies are attached to Battalions and Brigade Report Centre for this operation.

  (c) RED Ground Flares for communication with aeroplane will be carried, and lighted when called for by aeroplane. Special men in each platoon will be detailed for this purpose.

  (d) A Contact plane will fly over area of attack on 25th October.
      Flares will be called for at :-
      Zero plus 2½ hours, Zero plus 4½ hours.

  (e) Brigade Report Centre is established at CHLE LOUVIERE J.20.d.1.1.

13. HEADQUARTERS.
    Brigade Headquarters will be at NOYELLES-SUR-SELLE I.34.d.8.6.
    6th Black Watch   )
    6th A & S Highlanders.) BOLT FACTORY, J.15.c.5.3.
    7th Black Watch.   J.15.c.1.5.

12/.

- 3 -

13. (Continued).

    12th Canadian Infantry Brigade   ROUVIGNIES.
    6th Seaforth Highlanders.   QUARRY, J.28.a.central.

On capture of the GREEN LINE the following moves will take place :-

    Brigade Headquarters to BOLT FACTORY, J.15.c.5.3.
    6th Black Watch.   THIANT.
    6th A & S Highrs.   CHATEAU DES PRES, J.17.d.5.6.

14. REPORTS.
    Reports will be rendered to Brigade Headquarters every clock hour after ZERO.

15. PRISONERS OF WAR.
    Prisoners of War will be sent to Prisoners of War Cage DOUCHY.

16. MEDICAL ARRANGEMENTS.   will be notified later.

17. SYNCHRONISATION.
    A synchronised watch will be sent to all concerned at 02.00 hours today, 25th October.

18. ZERO HOUR.
    Zero hour will be at 07.00 hours, October, 25th.

19. ACKNOWLEDGE.

                                 Captain,
              Brigade Major 153rd Infantry Brigade.

ISSUED at 02.00 hours.
Copy No. 1 to 6th Black Watch.
       2   7th Black Watch.
       3   6th A & S Highlanders.
       4   153rd Trench Mortar Battery.
       5   "A" Coy. 51st M.G.Battalion.
       6   401st Field Coy. R.E.
       7   Brigade Signals.
       8   Staff Captain.
       9   War Diary.
      10   File.
      11   152nd Infantry Brigade.
      12   154th Infantry Brigade.
      13   12th Canadian Infantry Brigade.
      14   51st (Highland) Division "G".
      15   51st Divisional Artillery.
      16   51st M.G.Battalion.
      17   O.C. Cyclist Coy.
      18   Left Group Artillery.
      19   34th Brigade R.G.A.
      20   Brigade Gas Officer.

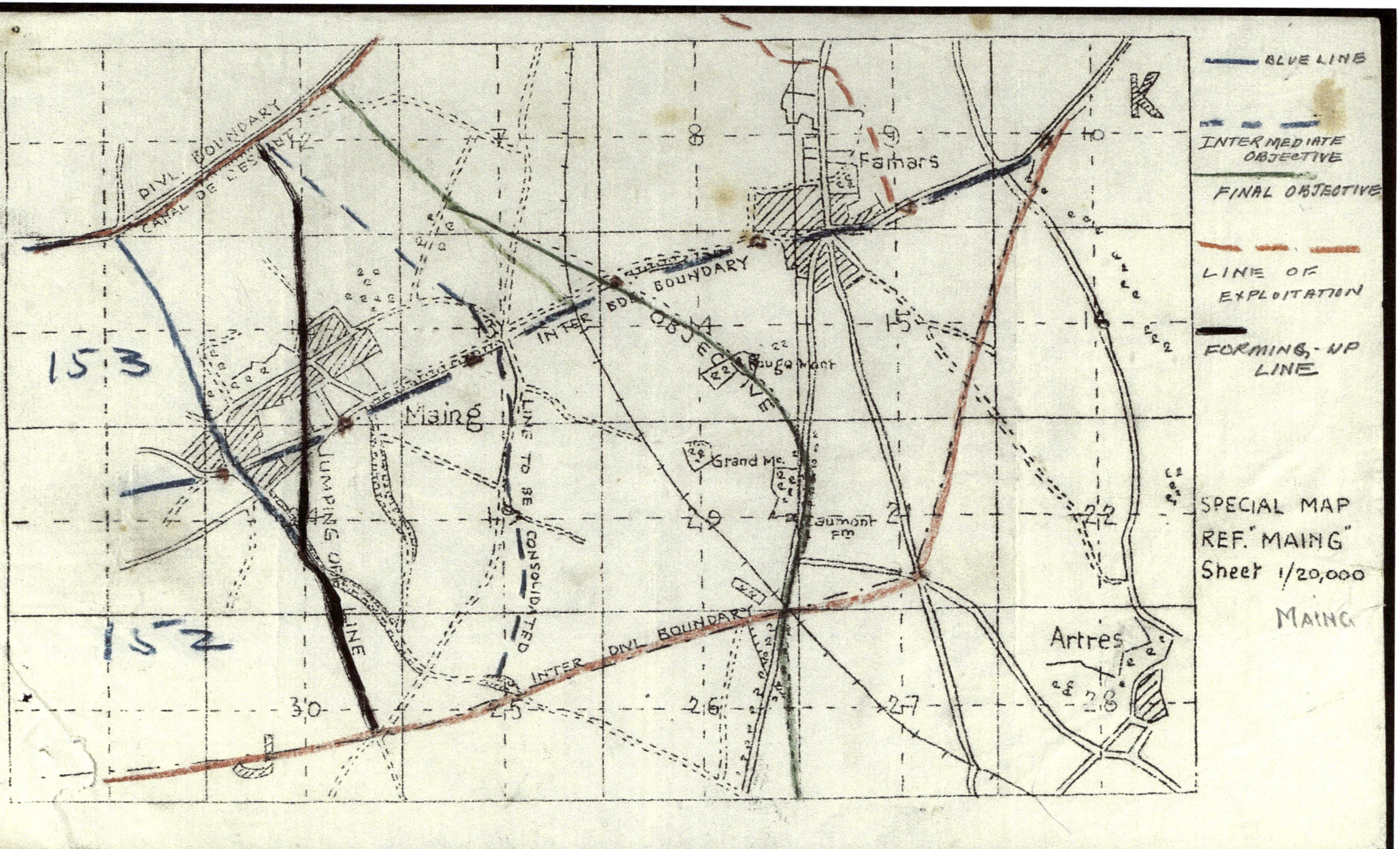
BLUE LINE
INTERMEDIATE OBJECTIVE
FINAL OBJECTIVE
LINE OF EXPLOITATION
FORMING-UP LINE
SPECIAL MAP
REF. "MAING"
Sheet 1/20,000
MAING
Famars
Maing
Artres
Rouge Mont
Grand Mc.
Caumont Fm
DIVL. BOUNDARY
CANAL DE L'ESCAUT
INTER BDE BOUNDARY
OBJECTIVE
LINE TO BE CONSOLIDATED
JUMPING OFF LINE
INTER DIVL BOUNDARY
153
152
K

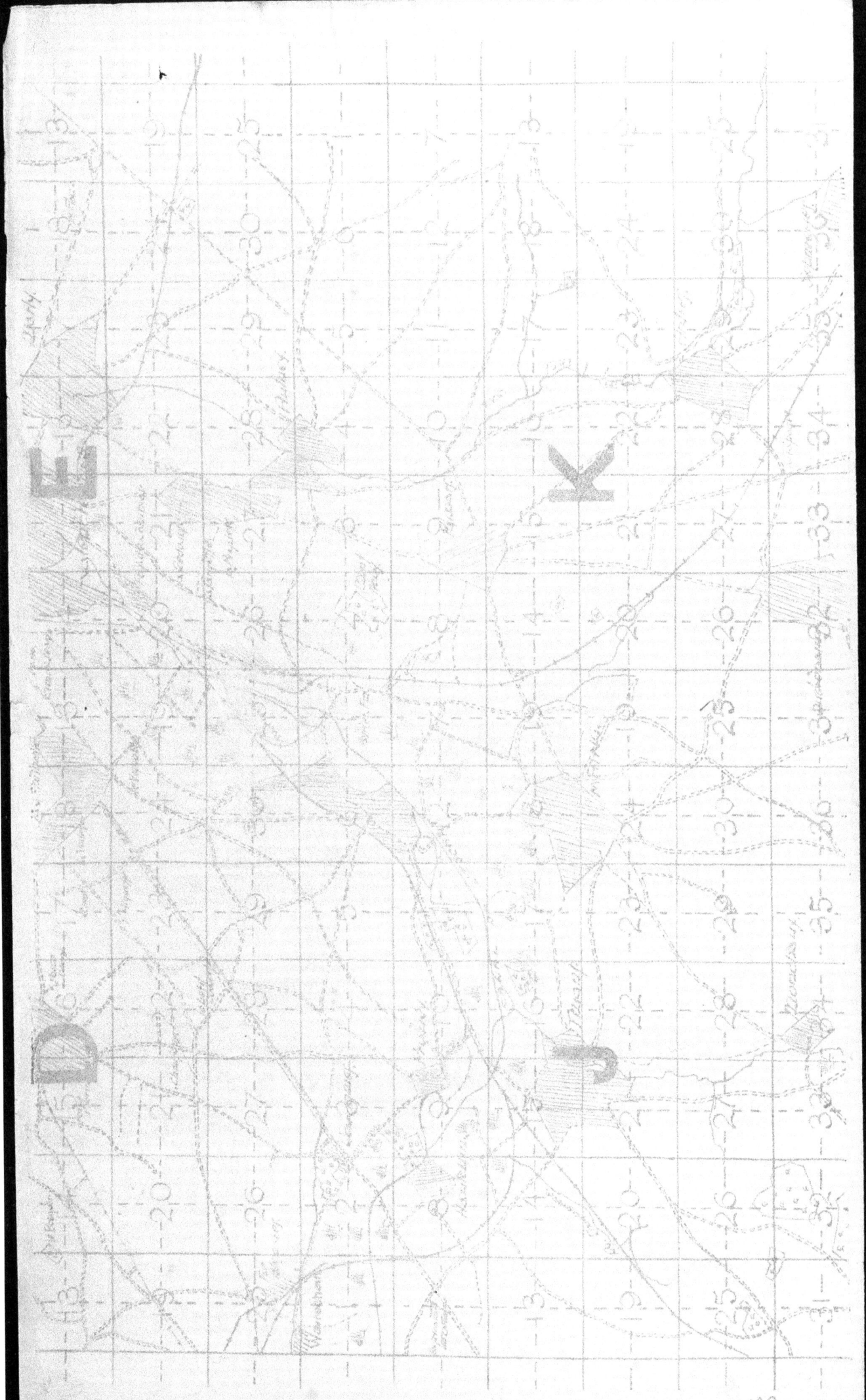

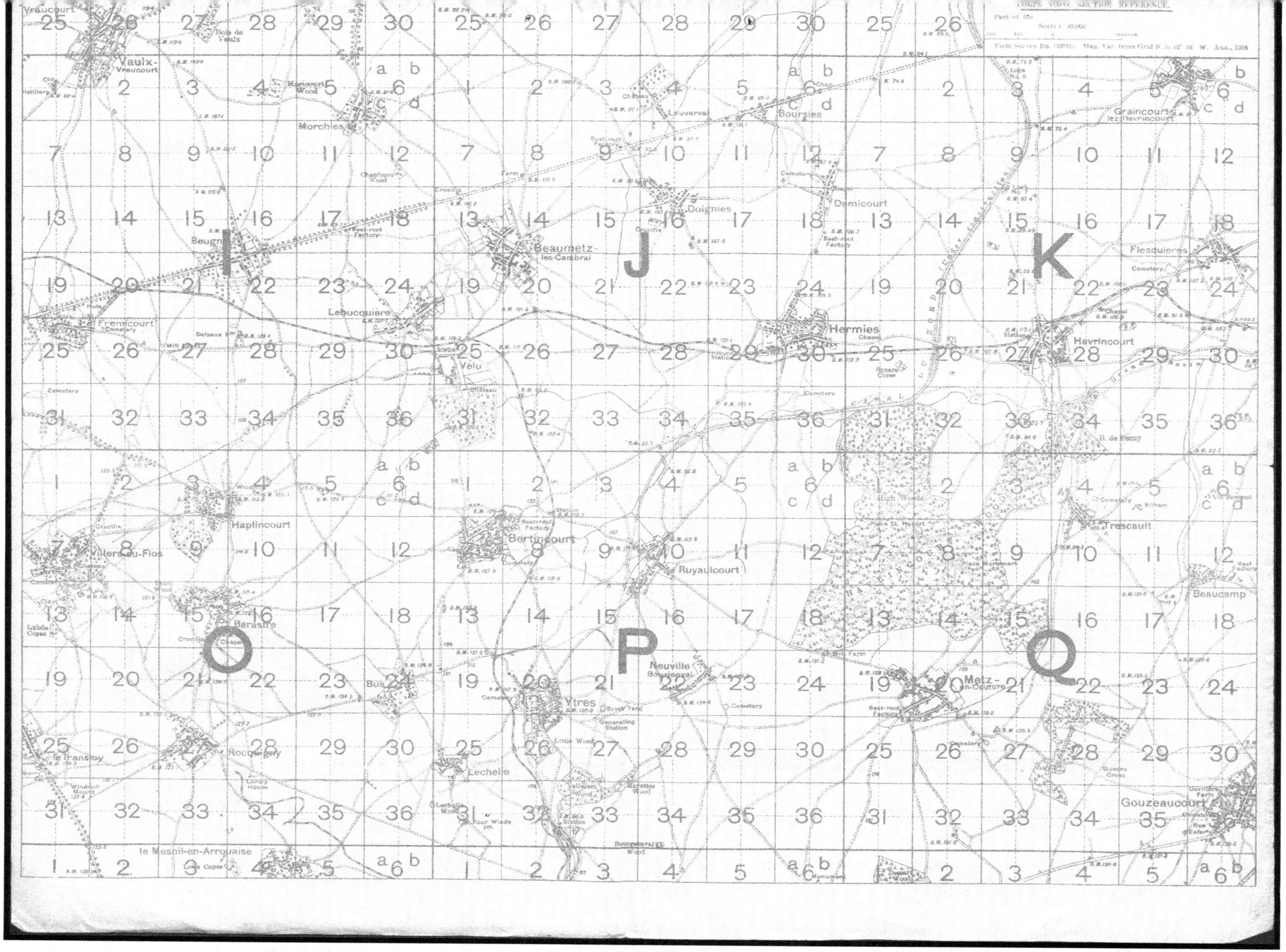
CORPS TOPO. SECTION REFERENCE.
Part of 57c
Scale 1 : 40,000
Field Survey Bn. (1078). Mag. Var. from Grid N. is 12° 16' W. Aug., 1918
I
J
K
O
P
Q
Vraucourt
Vaulx-Vraucourt
Morchies
Louverval
Boursies
Graincourt lez-Havrincourt
Demicourt
Coignies
Beaumetz-les-Cambrai
Flesquieres
Lebucquiere
Fremicourt
Hermies
Havrincourt
Velu
B. de Pemy
High Wood
Haplincourt
Bertincourt
Ruyaulcourt
Trescault
Villers-au-Flos
Beaucamp
Barastre
Neuville Bourjonval
Metz-en-Couture
Bus
Ytres
le Transloy
Rocquigny
Lechelle
Gouzeaucourt
le Mesnil-en-Arrouaise

"C" Form.
MESSAGES AND SIGNALS.

Army Form C. 2123.
(In books of 100.)

No. of Message _____

Prefix __ Code 2101 Words 48

Received. From BOPE By LOVE

Sent, or sent out. At ___ m. To ___ By ___

Office Stamp. TIWI 24/10/8

Charges to Collect

Service Instructions BOPE

Handed in at _____ Office _____ m. Received _____ m.

TO TIWI

*Sender's Number	Day of Month.	In reply to Number	AAA
DM 66	26		

Following message from General Carter Campbell AAA Please convey to Lt/Col Coats and all ranks of TIWI my congratulations on the fine fighting qualities displayed by the batt today AAA GOC has sent further congratulations by telephone on repulse of second counter-attack

FROM PLACE & TIME BOPE 2033

* This line should be erased if not required.

10th Bn. ARGYLL & SUTHERLAND HIGHRS.

ROLL OF OFFICERS.

Lt.Col.	S.	COATS, D.S.O.	Commanding Officer.
Major	H.McC.	McHAFFIE, M.C.	On leave.
Capt.	R.M.	ALLARDYCE.	O.C. "D" Coy.
Capt.	J.A.	KIRKWOOD.	
Capt.	J.A.	LATTA.	O.C. "B" Coy.
Capt.	D.	WATSON.	On leave.
A/Capt.	P.	HARRINGTON.	O.C. "C" Coy.
A/Capt.	A.	GARDINER.	Adjt.
Lieut.	J.H.	STOCKDALE.	Senior Transport Officer.
Lieut.	R.W.	TURNER.	Second-in-Command, "D" Coy.
Lieut.	J.B.	McGLASHAN.	
Lieut.	C.	FARQUHARSON.	Second-in-Command, "C" Coy.
Lieut.	J.W.	MUNRO.	O.C. "A" Coy.
Lieut.	J.D.	MILLER.	Sigs. Officer.
Lieut.	H.N.	WHIMSTER.	Asst. Adjt.
Lieut.	S.J.	MACKIN.	
Lieut.	A.	SHEARER.	On leave.
Lieut.	J.W.R.	PAINE.	Second-in-Command, "B" Coy.
Lieut.	J.F.	ADAM.	Asst. Gas-Off. (5th Div.)
Lieut.	G.J.	PIRIE.	On leave.
Lieut.	A.E.	MACGREGOR.	
Lieut.	A.	BROWN	
Lieut.	N.	MILLAR.	On leave.
Lieut.	J.J.	CRAWFORD.	
Lieut.	J.	ROBERTSON.	Course.
Lieut.	J.	MACPHIE.	
Lieut.	W.D.	BISSETT.	
Lieut.	J.	FERWICK.	
Lieut.	J.M.	DUFF.	
Lieut.	J.	GALBRAITH.	
2/Lieut.	M.W.	WARD.	
2/Lieut.	D.T.	BIRCH.	
2/Lieut.	J.P.	CAIRNS.	Transport Officer.
2/Lieut.	E.S.	BROWN.	On leave.
2/Lieut.	S.	FOULDS.	On leave.
Lt. & Q.M.	J.	SCAIFE, D.C.M.	Q.M.
Capt.		J.W.McELROY.	Medical Officer.
Capt.		J.J.HAWORTH.	Chaplain.

APP IV

SPECIAL   ORDER

by

Major-General G.T.C. Carter-Campbell, D.S.O.,

Commanding 51st (Highland) Division.

Saturday, 26th October, 1918.

The following message has been received by the General
Officer Commanding, from Lieut-General Sir A.J. Godley, K.C.B.,
K.C.M.G., Commanding XXII Corps, and is published for the
information of all ranks -

" The Corps Commander wishes to compliment the Division
" on their continued success of yesterday and today and
" would be glad if you would convey his special
" congratulations to the 1/6th Argyll & Sutherland
" Highlanders on their fine repulse of yesterday's
" counter attack. "

Alix Gordon

Lieut. Colonel,
A.A. & Q.M.G.

1/6th Bn. ARG. & SUTHD. HIGHRS.

FIGHTING STRENGTH.

REINFORCEMENTS.			WASTAGE.		
	O.	O.R.		O.	O.R.
Fighting strength, 30/9/18.	44.	963.	Killed,	1.	18.
From CCS.		6.	Died of wounds,		7.
From Recep. Camp, 1/10/18.		7.	Wounded,	2.	94.
From Base, 5/10/18.		2.	Acc. killed,		1.
" 14/10/18.	1.	17.	Sick,		53.
" 18/10/18.		1.	Missing,	1.	5.
" 21/10/18.		6.	Transferred,	3.	10.
" 29/10/18.		2.	Wounded (gas)	2.	
TOTAL,	45.	993.	Total,	9.	188.
WASTAGE,	9.	188.			
TOTAL,	36.	805.			

                                                                  Officers.   Other Ranks.

FIGHTING STRENGTH, 31/10/18.   36.   805.

                                                                            Lieut. Col.

31st October, 1918.   Commanding 1/6th A. & S. H.

WAR DIARY

OF THE

1/6TH BN. A. AND S. H.

FOR THE MONTH OF

NOVEMBER '18.

WAR DIARY
or
INTELLIGENCE SUMMARY.

(Erase heading not required.) 1/6th BN. ARGYLL SUTHERLAND HIGHLANDERS

Army Form C. 2118.

Volume XLII.

Place	Date	Hour	Summary of Events and Information	Remarks and references to Appendices
REF MAP. SHEET 51a S.W. 1/20,000 HORDAIN	1-11-18		BATTALION IN REST BILLETS IN VILLAGE OF HORDAIN. COYS. REORGANISING & GENERAL TRAINING. CAPT. J.A. LATTA TO L.G. COURSE AT G.H.Q. L.G. SCHOOL. LIEUT. J.W.R. PAINE ASSUMED COMMAND AND PAYMENT OF 'B' COY. CASUALTIES:- NIL.	/r
	2-11-18		BATTALION SITUATED & EMPLOYED AS ABOVE. THE FOLLOWING OFFICERS JOINED BN. FROM 31st (H) DIV. RECPT. CAMP AND WERE POSTED TO "C" COY:- LT. C. DyfC. B. DUNCAN, 2-LT. J.W. YOUNIE AND 2-LT. F.S.D. STEPHENSON. 27 O.R. ON LEAVE. 16 O.R. TO COURSE - L.G. & BOMBING - AT 22ND CORPS SCHOOL. 9 O.R. FROM BASE. CASUALTIES:- NIL	/r
	3-11-18		BATTALION SITUATED AS ABOVE. GENERAL TRAINING. THE FOLLOWING OFFICERS JOINED BN. FROM 31st (H) DIV. RECPT. CAMP:- 2-LT. J.E.V. LINDSEY "B" COY & 2ND LT. H.G. DAVIES "A" COY. MAJOR H. McCNICHAEFIE REJOINED FROM LEAVE & ASSUMED DUTIES OF 2ND IN COMMAND OF BN. LT. J. ROBERTSON FROM COURSE. DIVINE PARADE SERVICE - 11.30 A.M. CASUALTIES:- NIL.	/r
	4-11-18		BATTALION SITUATED AS ABOVE. GENERAL TRAINING - PLATOON - COY. IN ATTACK - LESSONS IN PAST OPERATIONS - RAPID ADVANCE - ADVANCE GUARDS, ETC. LT. J.J. CRAWFORD TO REST HOUSE, PARIS PLAGE. CASUALTIES:- NIL.	
	5-11-18		BATTALION SITUATED AND EMPLOYED AS ABOVE. CAPT. & ADJT. A. GARDINER & LIEUT. J.W. MUNRO GRANTED LEAVE TO PARIS. LIEUT. J.W.R. PAINE GRANTED ONE	/r

WAR DIARY
or
INTELLIGENCE SUMMARY.

Army Form C. 2118.

Volume XLII.

(Erase heading not required.) 1/7th Bn. ARGYLL & SUTHERLAND HIGHLANDERS.

Place	Date	Hour	Summary of Events and Information	Remarks and references to Appendices
REF. MAP. SHEET 51A S.W. 1/20,000 HORDAIN.	5-11-18		MONTHS LEAVE (SPECIAL) TO U.K. LT. J ROBERTSON & LT. J MACPHIE ASSUMED COMMAND OF PAYMENT OF "A" & "D" COYS. RESPECTIVELY. CASUALTIES:- NIL.	AA
	6-11-18		BATTALION SITUATED & EMPLOYED AS ABOVE. CASUALTIES:- NIL. A SPECIAL PARADE HELD AT VALENCIENNES.	AA App I.
	7-11-18		DO. LT. COL. S. COATS. O.S.O. TO COMMAND DETACHMENT FROM 22ND CORPS. WIRE RECEIVED THAT GERMAN PEACE ENVOYS PASSED THRO' OUR LINES TO G.H.Q. CASUALTIES:- NIL.	AA
	8-11-18		BATTALION SITUATED & EMPLOYED AS ABOVE. CASUALTIES:- NIL.	AA
	9-11-18		ALL OFFICERS & N.C.O'S (DOWN TO PLATOON COMMANDERS) ATTENDED A DEMONSTRATION GIVEN BY 6TH BN. R. HRDS. RE. "EXPLOITING THE ENEMY'S "SOFT SPOT". SHOWING HOW A FLANK CAN BE CREATED IN AN ENEMY LINE OF BATTLE. 2/LT. O.T. BIRCH & 24 O.R'S ON LEAVE. CAPT. J WATSON RETURNED OFF LEAVE & ASSUMED COMMAND & PAYMENT OF "B" COY. CASUALTIES:- NIL.	AA
	10-11-18		BATTALION SITUATED & EMPLOYED AS ABOVE. LIEUT. A BROWN JOINED 163RD TOL BATT. FOR DUTY. CASUALTIES:- NIL.	AA App 2
	11-11-18		HOSTILITIES CEASED - 11 A.M. BATTALION ON HOLIDAY. BON FIRE LIGHTED AT 6 P.M. & GREAT DISPLAY OF FIRE WORKS GIVEN BY ALL RANKS OF BATTALION. LT ROBERTSON TO COURSE 37TH ARMISTICE. DINNER AT BN. HQ. CASUALTIES:- NIL.	AA

WAR DIARY or INTELLIGENCE SUMMARY.

Army Form C. 2118.

Volume XLI.

(Erase heading not required.) 1/6TH BN. ARGYLL SUTHERLAND HIGHLANDERS

Place	Date	Hour	Summary of Events and Information	Remarks and references to Appendices
REF. MAP. SHEET. 27 S.W. 1/20,000.	12-11-18		BATTN. SITUATED AS ABOVE. GENERAL TRAINING. BRIG. GEN. W. GREEN, D.S.O. COMDG. 1/3RD. INF. BDE. INSPECTED TRANSPORT SECTION. CAPT. A.L. PATERSON. M.C. JOINED FOR DUTY FROM BASE. CASUALTIES:- NIL.	A.A.
	13-11-18		BATTN. SITUATED AS ABOVE. GENERAL TRAINING, PARTICULAR ATTENTION BEING PAID TO OPEN WARFARE, CEREMONIAL DRILL & MUSKETRY. CAPT. A.L. PATERSON. M.C. ASSUMED COMMAND OF PAYMENT OF "B" COY. CAPT. J.A. LATTA FROM COURSE. LIEUT. J.J. CRAWFORD FROM OFFICERS REST HOUSE. PARIS. PLACE. LT. C. FARQUHARSON ON LEAVE TO U.K. CASUALTIES:- NIL.	A.A.
	14-11-18		BATTALION SITUATED AS ABOVE. BATTALION PARADED AT 9AM & MARCHED TO FIELD N.W. OF IVILLY & CONFERRED BY THE PRESIDENT & REPUBLIC OF U.S. AMERICA. TO WITNESS PRESENTATION OF DECORATIONS UPON FIELD MARSHAL SIR D. HAIG. K.T. G.C.B. G.C.V.O. C.M.C. BRITISH ARMIES IN FRANCE. BY GEN. PERSHING. U.S.A. FORCES. CAPT. J.A. LATTA ASSUMED COMMAND OF PAYMENT OF "B" COY. VICE CAPT. A.L. PATERSON. M.C. LIEUT. G.J. PIRIE FROM LEAVE. CASUALTIES:- NIL	App 3. A.A.
	15-11-18		BATTALION SITUATED AS ABOVE. INSPECTION & ADDRESS BY MAJ. GEN. G.T.C. CARTER-CAMPBELL. D.S.O. LECTURE TO BN. BY REV. WM GILLIESON. S.C.F. ON "DEMOBILISATION". LT. J.F. ADAM REJOINED BN. FROM 5TH DIV. (ASSIST. DIV. GAS OFFICER.) CASUALTIES:- NIL.	A.A.

Army Form C. 2118.

WAR DIARY

VOLUME XLI

or

INTELLIGENCE SUMMARY.

(Erase heading not required) 10TH BN. ARGYLL SUTHERLAND HIGHLANDERS.

Place	Date	Hour	Summary of Events and Information	Remarks and references to Appendices
HORDAIN. REF. MAP. 51a S.W. 1/20,000	16-11-18		BATTALION SITUATED AS ABOVE. ROUTE MARCH, VIA LIEU ST AMAND. CAPT. R.M. DALRYMPLE ON LEAVE. LT. R.W. TURNER ASSUMED COMMAND & PAYMENT OF "D" COY. LT. J. ROBERTSON FROM COURSE. LT. N.D. BASSETT FROM HOSPITAL. 19 O.R. ON LEAVE TO U.K. LT. J.W. MUNRO FROM PARIS. CAPT. & ADJT. A. GARDINER FROM 1ST ARMY SCHOOL. CASUALTIES:- NIL	A6
✓	17-11-18		BATTALION SITUATED AS ABOVE. OPEN AIR DIVINE SERVICE AT 10.45. FIELD MARSHALL SIR D. HAIG K.T. G.C.B., G.C.V.O., K.C.I.E., C.IN.C. B.A. IN FRANCE & MAJ. GEN. G.T.C. CARTER-CAMPBELL D.S.O. C.MDG. 51ST (H) DIV PRESENT. INSPECTION OF TRANSPORT BY I.O.M. CASUALTIES:- NIL	A7
✓	18-11-18		BATTALION SITUATED AS ABOVE. RECREATIONAL TRAINING. INSPECTION BY CAPT. MACINTYRE OF ALL S.B.Rs. 2.LT. E.S. BROWN FROM LEAVE. CASUALTIES:- NIL	A8
✓	19-11-18		BATTALION SITUATED AS ABOVE. GENERAL & RECREATIONAL TRAINING. LT. A.E. McGREGOR FROM OFFRS. REST HOUSE PARIS PLAGE. COYS ON FORENOON PARADES ONLY. SPORTS DURING AFTERNOON. CASUALTIES:- NIL	A9
✓	20-11-18		BATTALION SITUATED AS ABOVE. A & B. COYS RANGE PRACTICE. C & D. COY. GENERAL TRAINING. CASUALTIES:- NIL	A9
✓	21-11-18		BATTALION SITUATED AS ABOVE. CROSS COUNTRY RUN. ROUTE MARCHES, ETC. LT. COL S. COATS. D.S.O. & LT. J. ROBERTSON ON LEAVE TO U.K. MAJ. McHAFFIE H. M.P.C. (O.I.C) ASSUMED COMMAND OF BN. CASUALTIES:- NIL	A9
✓	22-11-18		BATTALION SITUATED AS ABOVE. GENERAL & RECREATIONAL TRAINING. CAPT. J.A. LATTA TO PARIS ON LEAVE. CAPT. R.L. PATERSON. M.C. ASSUMED COMMAND & PAYMENT OF "B" COY. CASUALTIES:- NIL	A9

Army Form C. 2118.

WAR DIARY
or
INTELLIGENCE SUMMARY.

(Erase heading not required.) 1/6th Bn Argyll & Sutherland Highlanders.

Volume XLI.

Instructions regarding War Diaries and Intelligence Summaries are contained in F. S. Regs., Part II. and the Staff Manual respectively. Title pages will be prepared in manuscript.

Place	Date	Hour	Summary of Events and Information	Remarks and references to Appendices
HORDAIN REF. MAP 51° S.W. V100070	23-11-18		BATTALION SITUATED AS ABOVE. GENERAL & RECREATIONAL TRAINING. LT. J.D. MILLER VII O.R. ON LEAVE TO U.K. LIEUT. G.B. McGEE & DRAFT OF 78 O.R's JOINED FROM BASE. CASUALTIES:- 1 O.R. ACCID WOUNDED (REVOLVER SHOT)	JR
	24-11-18		BATTALION SITUATED AND EMPLOYED AS ABOVE. 2.LIEUT. F.S.D. STEPHENSON & 10 O.R. TO 1ST ARMY RIFLE SCHOOL. LIEUT. J. McPHIE TO OFFICERS REST HOUSE, PARIS PLAGE. CASUALTIES:- NIL.	JR
	25-11-18		BATTALION SITUATED & EMPLOYED AS ABOVE. CASUALTIES:- NIL.	JR
	26-11-18		do. CASUALTIES:- NIL.	JR
	27-11-18		do. A. & B. COYS AT RANGE PRACTICE. 2.LTS. S. FOULDS AND D.T. BIRCH FROM LEAVE. 2.LTS. J. HART & J.S. BROWNE AND 63 O.R's FROM BASE. LT. A.N. WHIMSTER ON LEAVE TO UK. ADMINISTRATIVE INSTRUCTIONS RECEIVED RE MOVE TO NEW AREA. CASUALTIES:- NIL.	JR
	28-11-18		BATTALION SITUATED AS ABOVE. COYS ROUTE MARCHING, CROSS COUNTRY RUNNING, ETC. CAPT. J.A. LATTA FROM PARIS & ASSUMED COMMAND & PAYMENT OF 'B' COY VICE CAPT. R.L. PATERSON, M.C. CASUALTIES:- NIL.	JR

WAR DIARY
or
INTELLIGENCE SUMMARY.

(Erase heading not required.) 1/6th Bn. ARGYLL & SUTHERLAND HIGHLANDERS

Army Form C. 2118.

Volume XLI

Place	Date	Hour	Summary of Events and Information	Remarks and references to Appendices
HORDAIN. REF. MAP S/o S.N. 1/20,000	29-11-18		BATTALION SITUATED AS ABOVE. COMPETITION BY COYS. "BEST DRILLED COY." JUDGED BY BRIG. GEN. W. GREEN, IN THE FOLLOWING ORDER:- "C" COY. (CAPT. P. HARRINGTON) "D" COY. (LT. A.W. TURNER), "A" COY. (CAPT. O. WATSON) "B" COY. (CAPT. J.A. LATTA). LT. A.E. MACGREGOR TO OXFORD FOR INSTRUCTION UNDER NEW EDUCATIONAL SCHEME. SUBJECT:- ENGLISH. DRAFT 16 OR's FROM BASE. CASUALTIES:-	A.1
	30-11-18		BATTALION SITUATED AS ABOVE. CAPT. J.A. LATTA TO LT. W.D. BISSET + 13 OR's ON LEAVE TO U.K. 51st (H) DIVISION SPORTS DAY NEAR ESTRUN. CASUALTIES:-	A.1

App.	Description.
1	Parades held at Valenciennes
2	Hostilities - ceasing of
3	Special Order - C. in C.
4	Fighting Strength
5	Roll of Officers.

[signature] Major
Lieut.-Col.
CMDG. 1 6th ARG. & SUTHRD HIGHRS

No. A.4300/1

PARADE

to be held at VALENCIENNES
at the Place Dame, on
Thursday, November 7th 1918

---

1. The Maire and Municipal Council of VALENCIENNES, having expressed their desire to thank the British Army for the liberation of their Town, a parade will be held as follows.-

   Representative detachments of as many units as possible from the XXII and Canadian Corps, will parade in the Place Dame, at 11.0 a.m., 7th November 1918.

2. Troops will form up facing HOTEL DE VILLE and on either flank.

   The detachment found by the XXII Corps will be on the right of the hollow square, viz:- half base and right side.

3. The detachment found by the XXII Corps will consist of 600 all ranks, and will be made up as follows :-

Detachment,	4th DIVISION.			170 strong.
"	49th "			170 "
"	51st "			170 "

   CORPS TROOPS, composed as follows, under the Command of Major C.E.HORNER, 193rd Siege Bty. RGA.

	Offr.	O.R.		
R.A.F.	1	9	10	"
Army F.A. Bdes) & Heavy Arty.)	2	28	30	"
Mounted Troops) & Cyclists.)	2	28	30	"
102nd M.G.Bn.	1	9	10	"
Labour.	1	9	10	"

   600 Strong.

4. The 51st Division will furnish a Pipe Band.

5. DRESS. Fighting order with steel helmets; all ranks dismounted.

6. The following will be the procedure :-

   (a) Army Commander arrives.
   (b) Troops will give general salute.
   (c) Address by the Maire and acknowledgment.
   (d) Inspection of troops.
   (e) After inspection, troops will present arms and the Band will play the "Marseillaise" and the "National Anthem."
   (f) Troops will march past in column of route and return to billets.

   P. T. C.

APP. 1.

(2)

7. Lieut.-Colonel S. COATS, 8th Bn. Argyll & Sutherland Highlanders, will command the troops of the XXII Corps. He will meet General ROSS at the HOTEL DU COMMERCE, VALENCIENNES, at 10 a.m., November 6th, to arrange details.

8. Markers will be on parade at 10.15 a.m.

   Troops will be in position at 10.30 a.m.

9. Divisional Commanders of the 4th, 49th, and 51st Divisions and their Staffs will meet the Corps Commander on the parade ground at the saluting base, at 10.45 a.m.

   All cars must be clear of the Square by 10.45 a.m.

   Lorries bringing troops will park in the Place de FAMARS.

   One Officer from each department of the Corps Staff will attend, if possible.

[signature]

Headquarters,
5th November 1918.

D. A. & Q. M. G.
XXII CORPS.

Copy to :- A.D.C. to Corps Commander.
4th Division.
49th "
51st "
G.O.C., R.A.
B.G., H.A.
XXII Corps Mounted Troops.
102nd M.G. Bn.
Labour Commandant.
52nd Squadron R.A.F.
Each Department of Corps Staff.
Major C.E. Horner, 193rd Siege Bty. RGA.
Lieut. Col. S. Coats, 6th A & S.H.

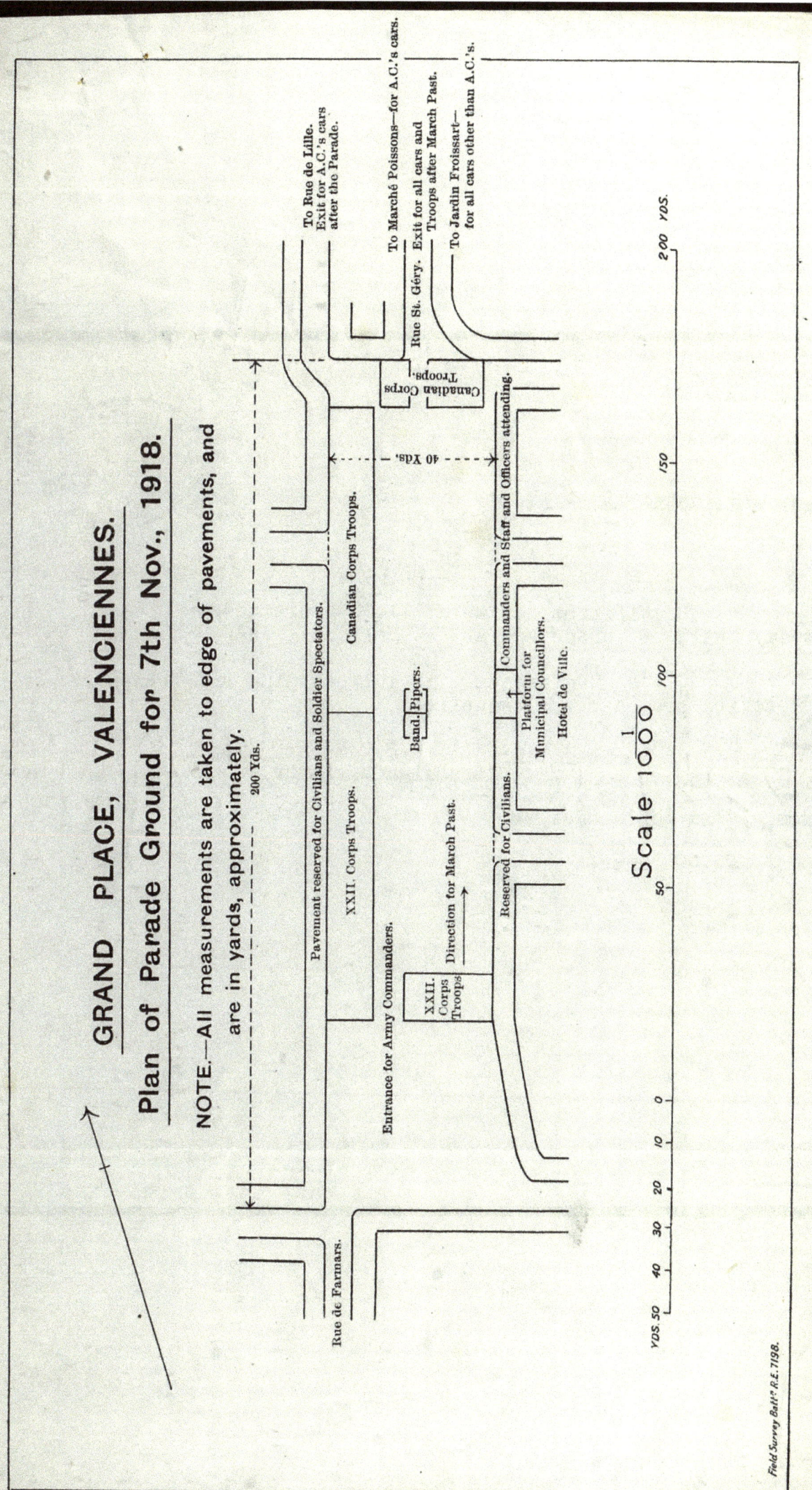

COPY.

B.M. 172 dated 11/11/18.

    Hostilities cease at 11.00 hours to-day AAA To-day will be observed as a Holiday AAA

    C.O's Conference for this evening and Transport Inspection are hereby cancelled.

                      (Sgd) W.P. MacNAB, Capt.
                        for Brigade Major.

From, 153rd Inf. Bde.

Time, 08.00 hours.

APP 2

COPY.

SPECIAL ORDER.

From Brigadier-General W. Green, D.S.O., Commdg. 153rd Inf. Bde.
To Lieutenant-Colonel S. Coats, D.S.O., Commdg. 1/6th A. & S. H.

"The Commander-in-Chief this morning asked me to convey to you his appreciation of the appearance of your Battalion and of their March Past.

The American Army Commander also complimented them on their turn-out.

Please inform all ranks."

14/11/18.
(Sgd) W. Green, Brig.-Gen.,
Commanding 153rd Infantry Brigade.

APP 3

1/6th BN. A. & S. HIGHRS.

FIGHTING STRENGTH.

REINFORCEMENTS.		O.	O.R.	WASTAGE.	O.	O.R.
Fighting Strength 31-10-18.		36	806.	Killed.	—	—
From Base.	1-11-18.	—	4.	Wounded.	—	2.
= =	2.	—	3.	Acc. Injured.	—	1.
= =	3	—	2.	Wounded.(Gassed.)	2.	55.
= =	5	—	2.	Sick. C.C.S.	—	34.
= =	8	—	2.	Transferd.	2.	10.
= =	10	—	2.	U.K. Commission.	—	1.
= =	12	1.	6.			
= =	13	—	2.			
= =	16	1.	1.			
= =	17.	1.	2.			
= =	18	—	3.			
= =	20	—	6.			
= =	21	—	3.			
= =	23	1.	82.			
= =	25	—	6.			
= =	27	2.	64.			
= =	29	—	16.			
= =	30	—	10.			
From S.C.S.	17	—	1.			
From 153 T.M.B.	17	—	2.			
TOTAL		47.	1019.	TOTAL.	4.	103.
WASTAGE		4.	103.			
TOTAL.		43.	916.			

                                          Officers. Other Ranks.

Fighting Strength. 30-11-18.   43.   916.

30th November, 1918.

                                              Major.
                        Comdg., 1/6th A. & S. H.

1/6th Bn. ARG. & SUTHD. HIGHRS.
ROLL OF OFFICERS.

Rank	Initials	Name	Notes
Lt.Col.	S.	COATS, DSO.	On leave.
Major.	H.McC.	McHAFFIE, M.C.	Commanding Officer.
Capt.	R.M.	ALLARDYCE.	On leave.
Capt.	J.A.	KIRKWOOD.	
Capt.	J.A.	LATTA.	On leave.
Capt.	D.	WATSON.	O.C. "A" Coy.
Capt.	A.L.	PATERSON, M.C.	O.C. "B" Coy.
A/Capt.	P.	HARRINGTON.	O.C. "C" Coy.
A/Capt.	A.	GARDINER.	Adjutant.
Lieut.	R.W.	TURNER.	O.C. "D" Coy.
Lieut.	C.	FARQUHARSON.	On leave.
Lieut.	G.B.	McGEE.	Joined 23/11/18. Second in Command, "C" Coy.
Lieut.	J.W.	MUNRO.	Btn. Educational Officer.
Lieut.	J.D.	MILLER.	On leave.
Lieut.	H.N.	WHIMSTER.	On leave.
Lieut.	S.J.	MACKIN.	Burial Officer.
Lieut.	A.	SHEARER.	
Lieut.	J.W.R.	PAINE.	On leave.
Lieut.	J.F.	ADAM.	Second in Command, "B" Coy.
Lieut.	G.J.	PIRIE.	Intelligence Officer
Lieut.	A.E.	MACGREGOR.	Course. Oxford.
Lieut.	N.	MILLAR.	On leave.
Lieut.	J.J.	CRAWFORD.	
Lieut.	J.	ROBERTSON.	On leave.
Lieut.	J.	MACPHIE.	Rest Camp.
Lieut.	W.D.	BISSETT.	
Lieut.	G.McC.B.	DUNCAN.	
Lieut.	J.	FENWICK.	
Lieut.	J.M.	DUFF.	
Lieut.	J.	GALBRAITH.	Transport Officer.
Lieut.	M.W.	WARD.	Second in Command, "A" Coy.
Lieut.	D.T.	BIRCH.	
Lieut.	J.P.	CAIRNS.	Leave.
Lieut.	E.S.	BROWN.	
2/Lieut.	S.	FOULDS.	
2/Lieut.	J.M.S.	BLAIR.	
2/Lieut.	H.G.	DAVIES.	
2/Lieut.	J.E.V.	LINDSAY.	
2/Lieut.	F.S.D.	STEPHENSON.	First Army Rifle School.
2/Lieut.	W.J.	YOUNIE.	Joined, 27/11/18.
2/Lieut.	J.S.	BROWNE.	-do-
2/Lieut.	J.	HART.	
Lt. & Q.M.	J.	SCAIFE, D.C.M.	Quartermaster.

Attached.

Rank	Initials	Name	Notes
Capt.	J.M.	FALKINER.	Medical Officer.
Capt.	J.J.	HAWORTH.	Chaplain.

McHaffie MAJOR,
LIEUT. COL.
CMDG. 1/6th ARG. & SUTHD HIGHRS

App. 5.

War Diary

of the

1/6th Bn. Arg. & Suth'd. Highrs.

for the month of

December - '18

WAR DIARY
or
INTELLIGENCE SUMMARY.

Army Form C. 2118.

Volume - XLIII.

10th Bn ARGYLL & SUTHERLAND HIGHLANDERS

Place	Date	Hour	Summary of Events and Information	Remarks and references to Appendices
HORDAIN, FRANCE. SHEET 51a S.W. 1/20,000.	1-12-18		BATTALION SITUATED AS STATED MARGINALLY. RECREATIONAL & GENERAL TRAINING. LT. J. MACPHIE REJOINED FROM REST HOUSE, PARIS PLAGE. LIEUT. J.P. CAIRNS ON LEAVE TO U.K. CAPT. A.L. PATERSON, M.C. ASSUMED COMMAND & PAYMENT OF "B" COY. LIEUT. J. GALBRAITH ASSUMED COMMAND & PAYMENT OF "TRANS. SECTION". CASUALTIES:- NIL.	
/	2-12-18		BATTALION SITUATED & EMPLOYED AS ABOVE. CASUALTIES:- NIL.	
/	3-12-18		do do INSPECTION OF BILLETS, KITS ETC. BY C.O. CAPT. J.A. KIRKWOOD ON LEAVE TO "NICE." 8 O.R ON LEAVE TO U.K. CASUALTIES:- NIL.	
/	4-12-18		BATTALION SITUATED & EMPLOYED AS ABOVE. REGIMENTAL COLOURS ARRIVED FROM PAISLEY UNDER CHARGE OF CAPT. R.M. PALARDYCE & MAJOR MACKEAN, TAKEN OVER BY THE FOLLOWING COLOUR ESCORT:- 2.LT. W.J. YOUNIE - 2.LT. H.C. DAWES - C.S.M. M^cDIARMID + 2 PRIVATES, WHICH MARCHED ROUND BN. H.Q. HEADED BY PIPE BAND. COLOURS WERE THEN TAKEN OVER BY PIPE MAJOR FINLAYSON & PLACED IN GUARD ROOM. LIEUT. N. MILLER FROM LEAVE. CASUALTIES:- NIL.	
/	5-12-18		BATTALION SITUATED & EMPLOYED AS ABOVE. CAPT. R.M. PALARDYCE & LIEUT. N. MILLER ASSUMED COMMAND & PAYMENT OF "D" COY. & TRANS. SECTION, RESPECTIVELY. CASUALTIES:- NIL.	

Army Form C. 2118.

WAR DIARY
or
INTELLIGENCE SUMMARY.

(Erase heading not required.) 6TH Bn ARGYLL & SUTHERLAND HIGHLANDERS

Volume XLIII.

Instructions regarding War Diaries and Intelligence Summaries are contained in F. S. Regs., Part II. and the Staff Manual respectively. Title pages will be prepared in manuscript.

Place	Date	Hour	Summary of Events and Information	Remarks and references to Appendices
HORDAIN FRANCE SHEET 51a S.W. 1/40,000	6-12-18		BATTALION SITUATED AS BEFORE. LT. COL. S. COATS. D.S.O. RETURNED FROM LEAVE. CASUALTIES:- NIL	
	7-12-18		do LT. COL. S. COATS D.S.O. ASSUMED COMMAND OF BN. MAJOR H. McC. McHAFFIE M.C. ASSUMED DUTIES OF 2ND IN COMMAND. CASUALTIES:- NIL	
"	8-12-18		BATTALION SITUATED AS BEFORE. DIVINE SERVICE IN CINEMA HALL. LIEUTS J. ROBERTSON & C. FARQUHARSON FROM LEAVE. CASUALTIES:- NIL	
"	9-12-18		BATTALION SITUATED AS BEFORE. EMPLOYED CLEARING THE FOLLOWING AREA OF SALVAGE. HORDAIN - BOUCHAIN - LIEU ST. AMAND - IWUY. LT. L.W.K. PAINE FROM LEAVE. CASUALTIES:- NIL	
"	10-12-18		BATTALION SITUATED & EMPLOYED AS BEFORE. CASUALTIES:- NIL	
"	11-12-18		do do LT. COL. S. COATS D.S.O. DETAILED AS COMMANDANT OF 22ND CORPS CONCENTRATION CAMP VALENCIENNES. MAJOR H. McC. McHAFFIE M.C. ASSUMED COMMAND OF BN. 9 MINERS RELEASED TO U.K. FOR WORK.	
"	12-12-18		BATTALION SITUATED & EMPLOYED AS BEFORE. 2 do do CASUALTIES:- NIL	
"	13-12-18		BATTALION SITUATED AS ABOVE. GENERAL RECREATIONAL TRAINING. 26 MINERS TO U.K. FOR WORK. LT. J. GALBRAITH CONDUCTING OFFICER. CASUALTIES:- NIL	

Army Form C. 2118.

WAR DIARY
INTELLIGENCE SUMMARY.

(Erase heading not required) 1/6th Bn. Argyll & Sutherland Highlanders

Volume XLIII

Instructions regarding War Diaries and Intelligence Summaries are contained in F. S. Regs., Part II. and the Staff Manual respectively. Title pages will be prepared in manuscript.

Place	Date	Hour	Summary of Events and Information	Remarks and references to Appendices
HORDAIN. FRANCE. SHEET 51a S.W. 1/20,000.	14-12-18		Battalion situated as per margin. General Training - Range Practice. Capt. J.A. Kirkwood from "Nice". Casualties:- Nil.	
	15-12-19		Battalion situated as above. Divine Services in Cinema Hall. Casualties:- Nil.	
	16-12-18		Battalion situated as above. General "Recreational Training. Capt. R.M. Allardyce assumed duties of 2nd in Command of Bn. Lt. R.W. Turner assumed command of "D" Coy. vice Capt. Allardyce. Lt. Whimster from leave. 2/Lieut. F.S.D. Stephenson from course. Casualties:- Nil.	
	17-12-18		Battalion situated as above. General "Recreational Training. Sailing. Capt. + Adjt. A. Gardiner + Lt. W.O. Bissett on leave. Capt. A.L. Paterson, M.C. to 51st (H) Div. H.Q. as Demobilization Officer. 5 miners to U.K. for work. Casualties:- Nil.	
	18-12-18		Battalion situated + employed as above. Lt. + Q.M. J. Schiff, D.C.M. on leave. Lt. H.N. Whimster assumed duties of Adjutant vice Capt. + Adjt. A. Gardiner. Lt. J.W.R. Paine assumed command of "B" Coy. vice Capt. A.L. Paterson, M.C. Casualties:- Nil.	
	19-12-18		Battalion situated + employed as above. Casualties:- Nil.	

Army Form C. 2118.

WAR DIARY
or
INTELLIGENCE SUMMARY.

(Erase heading not required.) 10TH BN ARGYLL & SUTHERLAND HIGHLANDERS

VOLUME XLIII

Instructions regarding War Diaries and Intelligence Summaries are contained in F.S. Regs., Part II. and the Staff Manual respectively. Title pages will be prepared in manuscript.

Place	Date	Hour	Summary of Events and Information	Remarks and references to Appendices
HORDAIN, FRANCE. SHEET 51b S.W. 1/20,000	20.12.18		Battalion situated & employed as before. Lt G.J. Pirie to Hospital. Casualties:- Nil.	
	21.12.18		Battalion situated & employed as before. Capt. P. Harrington & Lt J. Macphie, M.C. to Paris on leave. Lts J.W.R. Paine & C. Farquharson assumed command of B & C Coys. respectively on under orders for move to new area. Casualties:- Nil.	Anx 1
NEUVILLE L'ESCAUT, FRANCE. SHEET 51a S.W. 1/20,000	22.12.18		Battalion left Hordain 10am. Arrived Neuville L'Escaut 12noon. No Divine Service. Battn advised that Lt W.D. Bissett was awarded Victoria Cross by His Majesty the King. (See also further list attained - honours awarded) 2 miners to UK Release. Casualties:-	Anx 2
"	23.12.18		Battalion situated as above. General & Recreational Training. Casualties:- Nil.	
"	24.12.18		do do do Casualties:- Nil.	
"	25.12.18		do do Christmas Day observed as a Holiday. Lts. J.M. Duff & J.F. Adam from Paris leave. Casualties:- Nil.	

WAR DIARY or INTELLIGENCE SUMMARY.

Army Form C. 2118.

VOLUME XLIII.

1/6TH BN ARGYLL & SUTHERLAND HIGHLANDERS

Place	Date	Hour	Summary of Events and Information	Remarks and references to Appendices
NEUVILLE L'ESCAUT, FRANCE. SHEET 51a S.W. 1/20,000.	26-12-18		BATTALION SITUATED AS BEFORE. ROUTE MARCH: - BRESSEVILLE - NEUVILLE. LOUCHES - ROEULX - MASTAING - BOUCHAIN. CASUALTIES:- NIL.	
	27-12-18		BATTALION SITUATED AS ABOVE. RECREATIONAL TRAINING. LT J.F.ADAM + 2/LT R.S. BROWNE TO COURSE AT 1ST ARMY SCHOOL. CASUALTIES:- NIL.	
	28-12-18		BATTALION SITUATED AS ABOVE. GENERAL + RECREATIONAL TRAINING. "C" COY ON RANGE. 2/LT M.W. WARD ON LEAVE. CASUALTIES:- NIL.	
	29-12-18		BATTALION SITUATED AS ABOVE. DIVINE SERVICES IN VILLAGE CHURCH. CASUALTIES:- NIL.	
	30-12-18		BATTALION SITUATED AS ABOVE. GENERAL + RECREATIONAL TRAINING. CASUALTIES:- NIL.	
	31-12-18		BATTALION SITUATED AS ABOVE. HOLIDAY. CAPT P. HARRINGTON + LT J. MACPHIE, M.C. FROM PARIS. CASUALTIES:- NIL.	
			App 1. O.O. No 568.	
			" 2. AWARD - V.G. - LT W.D. BISSETT.	
			" 3. AWARDS TO O.R.S.	
			" 4. ROLL OF OFFICERS	
			" 5. STRENGTH STATE.	

Richards Capt Major
Lieut-Col.
CMDG. 1/6th ARG. & SUTH'D HIGH'RS

DIARY.

O.Cs,
A. B. C. D. Coys. H.Q.
Q.M., T.O., M.O.
H.Q., 153rd Inf. Bde. (For information).

---

1. The Battalion will move to NEUVILLE tomorrow 22nd inst.

2. The Battalion will be formed up ready to march at 10.00 hours, head of Column at Church, HORDAIN, facing IWUY.

3. Order of march - Signallers, Pioneers, Headquarters, "B" Coy, "C" Coy, "D" Coy, "A" Coy, Transport,. Guard and prisoners will march with Headquarters. 100 yards will be maintained between units.

4. The Colour Party will march in centre of "C" Coy, who will provide escort.

5. Blankets will be rolled in bundles of 10 and be piled at Orderly Room by 08.30 hours. Officers' valises and Mess kit at Orderly Room by 09.00 hours. Jerkins will be worn.

6. Billets and areas will be left clean, and certificates to that effect handed to Adjutant before marching off. Certificates from owners of billets that no damage chargeable to Battn. has been done, and that Mess premises have been paid for, will also be rendered.

7. O.Cs. Coys, H.Q. and Transport will report when all men are in billets on arrival.

8. Dinners will be cooked en route.

9. The new Battn. area will be bounded on the N.E. and S.W. by the last houses of the village of NEUVILLE at both ends, on the N.W. by the river, and on the S.E. by a line through X roads at the S.E. entrance to the village.

21/12/18.

Lieut.
A/Adjutant, 1/6th A. & S. Hrs.

1. **HONOURS AND REWARDS.**

His Majesty The King has been pleased to approve of the award of

THE VICTORIA CROSS

to Lieut. WILLIAM DAVIDSON BISSETT, (Renfrewshire) Bn. Argyll & Sutherland Highlanders, T.F. for most conspicuous bravery displayed on 25th October, 1918, during an attack on the Railway East of MAING.

Lieut. Bissett, when all the other officers in the Company had become casualties, took command although himself suffering from the effects of the continuous gas bombardment.

About 1600 hours, a determined counter attack degeloped against the left flank of his Company, which was exposed, and the enemy effected a lodgment behind it. Realizing the danger, he, with coolness and skill, withdrew the whole company to the Railway, thus temporarily saving the situation, but he then observed fresh bodies of the enemy coming on in large numbers. His men had exhausted their ammunition and further supplies were cut off by the barrage in rear. He therefore, sprang upon the Railway embankment, exposing himself to heavy machine gun fire, and called upon his men to charge with the bayonet, which they did.

The counter attack was shattered with great loss to the enemy, Lieut. Bissett himself shooting an entire machine gun crew with his revolver. He led the charge to a line beyond the original position from which he had withdrawn and finally reorganized the company upon it. During the performance of this duty he again exposed himself to heavy fire with complete disregard for his own safety.

By his fine leadership and splended example, Lieut. Bissett was the means of saving a critical situation, improving the position of our line and inflicting severe casualties upon the enemy.

The Corps and Divisional Commanders congratulate the recipient.

Authority:- XX11 Corps wire A.657 dated 21/12/18.

Capt. MAJOR
A/LIEUT.-COL.
CMDG. 1/6th ARG & SUTHND HIGHRS

DECORATIONS AWARDED SINCE THE BATTALION JOINED 51ST (HIGHLAND) DIVISION ON 5/10/18.

OFFICERS.

Capt. R.M. ALLARDYCE,		M.C.	Authy. 4th A.R.O. 3208
Lieut. J.W. MUNRO,		M.C.	dated 11/12/18.
Lieut. J. MACPHIE,		M.C.	

OTHER RANKS.

251252.	Sgt. J. DICKSON,	"A" Coy.	M.M. & Bar.	Authy. 51st D.R.O. 1140(1.B) dated 21/11/18 & C.R.O. 1845 dated 9/12/18.
326031.	Pte. J. BRYSON,	"B" Coy.	M.M.	Authy. 51st D.R.O. 1140 (1.B) dated 21/11/18.
252080.	Cpl. J. BLACKWOOD,	"D" Coy.	M.M.	do.
252395.	Pte. T. BENNETT,	"D" Coy.	M.M.	do.
250729.	Pte. J. McKEE,	"A" Coy.	M.M.	do.
251020.	Sgt. W. CUNNINGHAM,	"C" Coy.	M.M.	do.
251185.	L/Sgt. H. McNEIL,	"D" Coy.	M.M.	do.
251847.	Cpl. G. ROBERTSON,	"C" Coy.	M.M.	do.
252513.	Pte. T. SHAW,	"B" Coy.	M.M.	do.
200872.	Pte. S. KENDAL,	"C" Coy.	M.M.	do.
252116.	Sig. J. MALTMAN,	"D" Coy.	M.M.	do.
252450.	Sig. D. HENDERSON,	"D" Coy.	M.M.	do.
250946.	Pte. R. McKENZIE,	"B" Coy.	M.M.	do.
251545.	Pte. J. McBRIDE,	"B" Coy.	M.M.	do.
254052.	Pte. A. KENNEDY,	"A" Coy.	M.M.	do.
254016.	Pte. J. McKAY,	"B" Coy.	M.M.	do.
250671.	Pte. R. McNEIL,	"C" Coy.	M.M.	do.
252323.	Sig. C. TAYLOR,	"A" Coy.	M.M.	do.
251411.	Pte. G. BOYD,	"D" Coy.	M.M.	do.
202035.	Pte. E. PHILLIP,	"C" Coy.	M.M.	do.
325018.	L/Sgt. J. KILPATRICK,	"C" Coy.	M.M.	do.
250554.	Sgt. W. SLATER,	"D" Coy.	M.M.	do.
252087.	L/Sgt. C. WALLACE,	"A" Coy.	M.M.	do.
251103.	Pte. P. GALLOWAY,	"A" Coy.	M.M.	do.
251434.	Sig. S. JONES,	"D" Coy.	M.M.	do.
251043.	Sig.L/Cpl. J. ALLAN,	"C" Coy.	M.M.	do.
250885.	Sig. S. KELLOCK,	"C" Coy.	M.M.	do.
252405.	Pte. J. BONNAR,	"C" Coy.	M.M.	do.
325468.	Pte. D. KENNEDY,	"D" Coy.	M.M.	do.
202809.	Pte. L. WOODINGTON,	"D" Coy.	M.M.	do.
253963.	Pte. D. WILKIE,	"D" Coy.	M.M.	do.
251052.	Pte. W. CLABBURN,	"D" Coy.	M.M.	do.
251974.	Pte. G. WATKINS,	"A" Coy.	M.M.	do.
251284.	Pte. R. FAIRLIE,	"A" Coy.	M.M.	do.
251954.	Pte. M. CORCORAN,	"A" Coy.	M.M.	do.
251110.	A/L/Cpl. W. PATON,	"A" Coy.	M.M.	51st D.R.O. 1157 (1(ii) dated 13/12/18.
251641.	A/L/Cpl. C. MILLAR,	"D" Coy.	M.M.	do.
251001.	Pte. J.D. WALKER,	"C" Coy.	M.M.	do.
251771.	Sgt. A. SINCLAIR,	"C" Coy.	D.C.M.	Authy. 4th A.R.O. 3209 dated 11/12/18.

R.M. Allardyce Capt.
MAJOR
LIEUT.-COL.
CMDG. 1/6th ARG. & SUTHND HIGHRS

1/6TH BN. ARG. & SUTHD. HIGHRS.
ROLL OF OFFICERS.

Rank	Initials	Name	Duty
Lt.Col.	S.	COATS, D.S.O.	XXII Corps Concentration Camp.
Major.	H.McC.	McKENZIE, M.C.	Commanding Officer.
Capt.	R.M.	ALLARDYCE, M.C.	Second-in-Command.
Capt.	J.A.	KIRKWOOD.	2nd-in-Command "A" Coy.
Capt.	J.A.	LATTA.	On leave.
Capt.	D.	WATSON.	O.C. "A" Coy.
Capt.	A.L.	PATERSON, M.C.	Div. Demobilizing Officer.
A/Capt.	P.	HARRINGTON.	O.C. "C" Coy.
A/Capt.	A.	GARDINER.	Adjutant. On leave.
Lieut.	R.W.	TURNER.	O.C. "D" Coy.
Lieut.	C.	FARQUHARSON.	2nd-in-Command "C" Coy.
Lieut.	G.B.	McGEE.	
Lieut.	J.W.	MUNRO, M.C.	Btn. Education Officer.
Lieut.	J.D.	MILLER.	On leave.
Lieut.	H.H.	WHIMSTER.	Actg. Adjutant.
Lieut.	S.J.	MACKIN.	Div. Salvage Officer.
Lieut.	A.	SHEARER.	Btn. Imprest Holder.
Lieut.	J.W.R.	PAINE.	O.C. "B" Coy.
Lieut.	J.F.	ADAM.	1st Army Inf. School.
Lieut.	G.J.	PIRIE.	HOSPITAL.
Lieut.	A.B.	MACGREGOR.	Course – Oxford.
Lieut.	N.	MILLAR.	Transport Officer.
Lieut.	J.J.	CRAWFORD.	
Lieut.	J.	ROBERTSON.	
Lieut.	J.	MACPHIE, M.C.	2nd-in-Command "B" Coy.
Lieut.	W.D.	BISSETT, V.C.	On leave.
Lieut.	C.McC.B.	DUNCAN.	Billet Party.
Lieut.	J.	FENWICK.	Leave.
Lieut.	J.M.	DUFF.	
Lieut.	J.	GALBRAITH.	Conducting Officer – Coal Miners.
Lieut.	M.W.	WARD.	Leave.
Lieut.	D.T.	BIRCH.	
Lieut.	J.P.	CAIRNS.	
Lieut.	E.S.	BROWN.	
2/Lieut.	S.	FOULDS.	Town Major – New Area.
2/Lieut.	J.M.S.	BLAIR.	2nd-in-Command "D" Coy.
2/Lieut.	R.S.	BROWNE.	1st Army Rifle School.
2/Lieut.	H.C.	DAVIES.	
2/Lieut.	J.	HART.	
2/Lieut.	J.E.V.	LINDSAY.	
2/Lieut.	F.S.D.	STEPHENSON.	
2/Lieut.	W.J.	YOUNIE.	
Lt. & Q.M.	J.	SCAIFE, D.C.M.	Quartermaster – Leave.

Attached.

Rank	Initials	Name	Duty
Capt.	R.M.	FAIRLIEFF.	Medical Officer.
Capt.	J.J.	HAWORTH.	Chaplain.

MAJOR,
LIEUT.-COL.
CMDG. 1/6th ARG. & SUTHND HIGHRS

1/6TH BN. ARG. & SUTHD. HIGHRS.

FIGHTING STRENGTH.

3 - JAN. 1919

REINFORCEMENTS.		O.	O.R.	WASTAGE.	O.	O.R.
Fighting Strength.	30/11/18.	43	916	Sick. C.C.S.	-	24
From Base.	2/12/18.	-	5	Transferred.	-	10
" "	3	-	4	Released.		47
" "	6	-	4			
" "	11	-	16			
" "	13	-	5			
" "	14	-	9			
" "	17	-	3			
" "	24	-	13			
" C.C.S.			3			
TOTAL		43	978.	TOTAL.	X	81
WASTAGE.		-	81			
TOTAL.		43	897.			

Major
~~LIEUT. COL.~~
CMDG. 1/6th ARG. & SUTHND HIGHRS

App 5

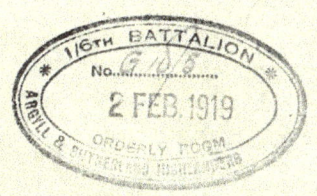

War Diary

of the

1/6th Bn. A & S. H.

for the month of

January - 1918

WAR DIARY
or
INTELLIGENCE SUMMARY.
(Erase heading not required.) 6th Batn. Argyll & Sutherland Highlanders

Army Form C. 2118.

Volume XLIV.

Place	Date	Hour	Summary of Events and Information	Remarks and references to Appendices
NEUVILLE L'ESCAUT FRANCE SHEET 51/9 S.W. 1/20 000	1-1-19		Battalion situated as per margin. Holiday. Capt. P. Harrington assumed command of "C" Coy. Casualties:- 10.R. Acci. killed.	19
	2-1-19		Battalion situated as above. Holiday. Casualties:- Nil.	19
	3-1-19		Battalion situated as above. Employed general clean up etc. Casualties:- Nil.	19
	4-1-19		Battalion situated as above. Saturday - Holiday. Capt. & Adjt. A. Gardiner from leave. Casualties:- Nil.	19
	5-1-19		Battalion situated as above. Divine Services in Church & School room. Casualties:- Nil.	19
	6-1-19		Lt. J. Galbraith from leave. Battalion situated as above. Training - General. Casualties:- Nil.	19
	7-1-19		Battalion situated as above. Training - General. Casualties:- Nil.	19
	8-1-19		Battalion situated as above. Preparing for move to new area. Transport moved by road. Casualties:- Nil.	19
	9-1-19		Bn. embussed at 11am at Freyte-au-Porier on the main Cambrai -	19

Army Form C. 2118.

WAR DIARY
or
INTELLIGENCE SUMMARY.
(Erase heading not required.) 1/10th Bn Argyll & Sutherland Highlanders

Volume XLIV.

Instructions regarding War Diaries and Intelligence Summaries are contained in F. S. Regs., Part II. and the Staff Manual respectively. Title pages will be prepared in manuscript.

Place	Date	Hour	Summary of Events and Information	Remarks and references to Appendices
	9.1.19		VALENCIENNES ROAD & TRAVELLED TO BOIS D'HAINE VIA THE FOLLOWING ROUTE:- DOUCHY, ROUVIGNIES, VALENCIENNES, MONS, MANAGE. MARCHED FROM MANAGE TO BILLETS AT BOIS D'HAINE ARRIVING AT 5 P.M. LT. J.J. CRAWFORD ON LEAVE TO UK. CASUALTIES:- NIL	N/A
BELGIUM. BOIS D'HAINE. SHEET 6. BRUSSELS. SET "C" 1/100,000	10.1.19		BATTALION SITUATED AS ABOVE. BN. RESTING & ARRANGING BILLETS. TRANSPORT ARRIVED ABOUT 4 P.M. CASUALTIES:- NIL	N/A
	11.1.19		BATTALION SITUATED AS ABOVE. RECREATIONAL TRAINING. LT. J.J. PIRIE FROM HOSPITAL CASUALTIES:- NIL	N/A
	12.1.19		BATTALION SITUATED AS ABOVE. DIVINE SERVICES IN VILLAGE CHURCH. LIEUT. J.W. MUNRO, M.C. ON LEAVE. LT. C. FARQUHARSON ASSUMED DUTIES OF BN. EDUCATION OFFICER. CASUALTIES:- NIL	N/A
"	13.1.19		BATTALION SITUATED AS ABOVE. RECREATIONAL TRAINING. CASUALTIES:- NIL	
"	14.1.19		do do do	
"	15.1.19		do do do	
"	16.1.19		do do 2/LT. H.C. DAVIES & 2/LT. J.E.V. LINDSAY, 3 DAYS LEAVE TO BRUSSELS. LT. M.W. WARD FROM LEAVE. CASUALTIES:- NIL	
"	17.1.19		BATTALION SITUATED AS ABOVE. GENERAL RECREATIONAL TRAINING. LT. W.D. BISSETT, V.C. FROM LEAVE	N/A

WAR DIARY
or
INTELLIGENCE SUMMARY.

(Erase heading not required.) 10th Bn ARGYLL SUTHERLAND HIGHLANDERS

Army Form C. 2118.

VOLUME XLIV

Place	Date	Hour	Summary of Events and Information	Remarks and references to Appendices
BOIS D' HAINE, BELGIUM. SHEET 6 BRUSSELS SET "C" 1/100 000	18.1.19		BATTALION SITUATED AS ABOVE. HOLIDAY. LT. W.D. BISSETT. V.C. TO HOSPITAL. CASUALTIES:- NIL.	A.
	19.1.19		BATTALION SITUATED AS ABOVE. DIVINE SERVICES IN VILLAGE CHURCH & HALL. CASUALTIES:- NIL.	A.
	20.1.19		BATTALION SITUATED AS ABOVE. GEN & RECREATIONAL TRAINING. CASUALTIES:- NIL	
	21.1.19		do do	
	22.1.19		do do	
	23.1.19		do do 2/Lt R.S. WARSHINE FROM COURSE	
	24.1.19		do do	
	25.1.19		do do HOLIDAY 7 OR's TO UK DEMOB. do LT. W.D. BISSETT V.C. FROM HOSPITAL	A.
	26.1.19		do DIVINE SERVICES IN VILLAGE CHURCH & HALL. do LT. L. FARQUHARSON 12 UK DEMOBILIZED AND 90 OTHER RANKS LT A.G. MACGREGOR, BN. SCOUT OFFR. VICE LT. FARQUHARSON	A.
	27.1.19		do NO TRAINING OWING TO FROST do CAPT. R.M. ALLBROOKE MC/ND UK. DEPOB.	
	28.1.19		do do do CAPT. J.A. KIRKWOOD ASSUMES DUTIES OF S. IN C. OF BN. VICE CAPT. ALLBROOKE M.C.	A.
	29.1.19		BATTALION SITUATED AS ABOVE. H.R.H. PRINCE OF WALES VISITED BN. INTRODUCED TO ALL OFFICERS OF BN. IN H.B. MESS. INSPECTED BAND & ALL MEN WITH DECORATIONS. CASUALTIES:- NIL.	A.

WAR DIARY or INTELLIGENCE SUMMARY

Army Form C. 2118.

Volume XLIV

6th Bn Argyll Sutherland Highlanders

Place	Date	Hour	Summary of Events and Information	Remarks and references to Appendices
BELGIUM. Bois D'Haine Sheet 6	20-1-19		Battalion situated as per margin. General "Recreational" Training. Lt J.J. Crawford from leave. Casualties:- Nil	K.
Brussels Sey "C" Hum.000	31-1-19		Battalion situated as above. General Recreational Training. Capt. D. Watson on leave- Rouen. Auth. of G.O.C. given for Major H. McIlcharsie M.C. to near bridges of Kain or Leitz. Col. Muir Commanding 10th Bn. A & S.H.	M.

App 1. Roll of Officers
App 2. Fighting Strength

[signature] LIEUT.-COL.
CMDG. 1/6th Arg. & Suthd. Highrs

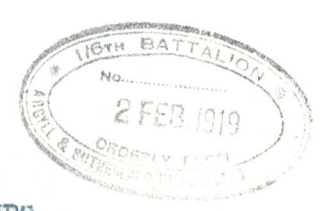
2 FEB 1919

1/6TH BN. ARG. & SUTHD. HIGHRS.

ROLL OF OFFICERS.

Lt.Col.	S.	COATS, D.S.O.	Brigade H.Q.
Lt.Col. ~~Major~~	H.McC.	McHAFFIE, M.C.	Commanding Officer.
Capt.	J.A.	KIRKWOOD.	Second-in-Command.
Capt.	J.A.	LATTA.	On leave.
Capt.	D.	WATSON.	~~O.C. "A" Coy.~~ LEAVE
Capt.	A.L.	PATERSON, M.C.	Div. Demobilization Officer.
A/Capt.	P.	HARRINGTON, M.C.	On leave.
A/Capt.	A.	GARDINER.	Adjutant.
Lieut.	R.W.	TURNER.	O.C. "D" Coy.
Lieut.	G.B.	McGEE.	O.C. "C" Coy.
Lieut.	J.W.	MUNRO, M.C.	On leave.
Lieut.	H.N.	WHIMSTER.	A/Adjutant.
Lieut.	S.J.	MACKIN.	Div. Salvage Officer.
Lieut.	A.	SHEARER.	Btn. Imprest Holder.
Lieut.	J.W.R.	Paine.	O.C. "B" Coy.
Lieut.	J.F.	ADAM.	1st Army Inf. School.
Lieut.	G.J.	PIRIE.	Intelligence Officer.
Lieut.	A.E.	MACGREGOR, M.C.	2nd-in-Command "D" Coy.
Lieut.	N.	MILLAR.	Transport Officer.
Lieut.	J.J.	CRAWFORD.	~~On leave.~~ O.C. "A" Coy.
Lieut.	J.	ROBERTSON.	Paris Plage - Rest House.
Lieut.	J.	MACPHIE, M.C.	2nd-in-Command "B" Coy.
Lieut.	W.D.	BISSETT, V.C.	2nd-in-Command "C" Coy.
Lieut.	C.McC.B.	DUNCAN.	Leave - Paris.
Lieut.	J.	FENWICK.	On leave.
Lieut.	J.M.	DUFF.	
Lieut.	D.T.	BIRCH.	
Lieut.	M.W.	WARD.	
Lieut.	J.P.	CAIRNS.	
Lieut.	E.S.	BROWN.	
2/Lieut.	S.	FOULDS.	Town Major, BOIS D' HAINE.
2/Lieut.	J.M.S.	BLAIR.	
2/Lieut.	R.S.	BROWNE.	
2/Lieut.	H.C.	DAVIES.	MANAGE Rail Guard.
2/Lieut.	J.	HART.	
2/Lieut.	J.E.V.	LINDSAY.	
2/Lieut.	F.S.D.	STEPHENSON.	
2/Lieut.	W.J.	YOUNIE.	
Lt.& Q.M.	J.	SCAIFE, D.C.M.	Quartermaster.

Attached.

Capt.	J.M.	FALKINER.	Medical Officer.

1/6TH BN. ARG. & SUTHD. HIGHRS.

FIGHTING STRENGTH.

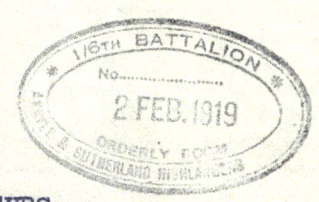

REINFORCEMENTS.				WASTAGE.		
		O.	O.R.		O.	O.R.
Fighting strength. 31/12/18.		43	897.	Sick. C.C.S.	–	26
From Base. 6/1/19.		–	9	Demobilized.	–	22
" " 8		–	6	Died.	–	1
" " 13		–	2	Base Clerks.	–	2
" " 19		–	20	Struck off (on leave)	1	–
" " 23		–	1			
From C.C.S.		–	4			
TOTAL.		43	939	TOTAL.	1	51
WASTAGE.		1	51			
	TOTAL.	42	888			

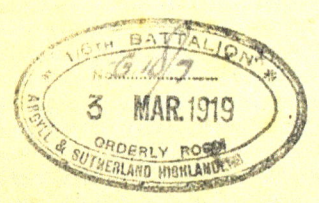

WAR DIARY

OF THE

1/6th Bn. Arg. & Suth'd. Highrs

FOR THE MONTH OF

FEBRUARY 19.

Army Form C. 2118.

WAR DIARY
or
INTELLIGENCE SUMMARY.

(Erase heading not required.) 10th Bn ARGYLL & SUTHERLAND HIGHLANDERS.

Volume XLV.

Instructions regarding War Diaries and Intelligence Summaries are contained in F. S. Regs., Part II. and the Staff Manual respectively. Title pages will be prepared in manuscript.

Place	Date	Hour	Summary of Events and Information	Remarks and references to Appendices
BELGIUM. BOIS D'HAINE. SHEET S27 "C" 1/100,000	1-2-19		BATTALION SITUATED AS PER MARGIN. HOLIDAY. Lt. J.J. CRAWFORD ASSUMED COMMAND OF "A" COY VICE CAPT. D. WATSON. CASUALTIES:- Nil.	N.
	2-2-19		BATTALION SITUATED AS ABOVE. DIVINE SERVICES IN VILLAGE CHURCH & HALL. Lt. C McB. DUNCAN FROM PARIS. CASUALTIES:- Nil	N.
	3-2-19		BATTALION SITUATED AS ABOVE. GENERAL & RECREATIONAL TRAINING. CASUALTIES:- Nil	N.
	4-2-19		do do do do do	
	5-2-19		do do do do Lt J.W.R. PAINE	N.
			* Lt E.S. BROWN TO BRUSSELS. Lt J.M. DUFF RESUMED COMMAND OF "B" COY. VICE Lt. J.W.R. PAINE.	
	6-2-19		BATTALION SITUATED & EMPLOYED AS ABOVE. Lt J MACPHIE M.C. Lt A.N. WHIMSTER, & Lt D.T. BIRCH & 75 ORS. PROCEEDED FOR DEMOBILIZATION. CASUALTIES:- Nil	N.
	7-2-19		BATTALION SITUATED & EMPLOYED AS ABOVE. CASUALTIES:- Nil	
	8-2-19		HOLIDAY. Lt J.M. DUFF & CAPT. J.A. KIRKWOOD & 450 O.R's PROCEEDED FOR DEMOBILIZATION. ⅋Capt J.W.R. PAINE & Lt E.S. BROWN FROM BRUSSELS. ⅋Capt J.W.R. PAINE ASSUMED COMMAND OF "B" COY. CASUALTIES:- Nil	N.
	9-2-19		BATTALION SITUATED AS ABOVE. DIVINE SERVICES IN VILLAGE CHURCH & HALL. CASUALTIES:- Nil	

WAR DIARY
or
INTELLIGENCE SUMMARY.

Army Form C. 2118.

(Erase heading not required.) 1/10th Bn ARGYLL & SUTHERLAND HIGHLANDERS

Volume XLV

Place	Date	Hour	Summary of Events and Information	Remarks and references to Appendices
BELGIUM BOIS D'AINE SHEET 6 BRUSSELS SET "C" 1/100,000	10.2.19		Battn. situated & employed as before. Lt. J.W. Munro, M.C. from leave. Casualties:- Nil.	
	11.2.19		do do do	
	12.2.19		do do Lts. G.J. Parie & J.W.R. Paine 1914 O.R.s proceeded for demobilization. Casualties:- Nil. Lt. J.W.R.	
	13.2.19		Battn. situated & employed as before. Lt. E.S. Brown assumed command of "B" Vice Lt. J.W.R. Paine. 12 O.R.s proceeded for demobilization. Casualties:- Nil.	
	14.2.19		Battn. situated & employed as before. Capt. D. Watson from Rouen. Lt. I. Robertson & A.E. McGregor, M.C. & 29 O.R.s proceeded for demobilization. Capt D. Watson assumed command of "A" Coy. Casualties:- Nil.	
	15.2.19		Battn. situated as above. Holiday. 25 O.R.s proceeded for demobilization. Casualties:- Nil.	
	16.2.19		do do Divine Services in Village Church & Hall. Casualties:- Nil.	
	17.2.19		do 2/Capt. P. Harrington M.C. returned from leave & assumed command of "C" Coy. Battalion situated as above. General & Recreational Training. Casualties:- Nil.	
	18.2.19		do do do do do C/Sgt G.B. McGee to Hos. do	
	19.2.19		do do do do do Lt (A/Capt.) A.W. Turner on leave. 2/Lt. J.D.L.S. Blair assumed command of "D" Coy. 53 O.R.s proceeded for demob. Lt. C. Mc & B. Duncan. The following officers proceeded as draft conducting officers:- Lt. C. Mc & B. Duncan. 2/Lt. F.S.D. Stephenson & 2/Lt. W.J. Younie. Lt. G.B. McGee to Hospital. Casualties:- Nil.	

Army Form C. 2118.

WAR DIARY
or
INTELLIGENCE SUMMARY.
(Erase heading not required) 10TH BN ARGYLL & SUTHERLAND HIGHLANDERS.

VOLUME XLV.

Instructions regarding War Diaries and Intelligence Summaries are contained in F. S. Regs., Part II. and the Staff Manual respectively. Title pages will be prepared in manuscript.

Place	Date	Hour	Summary of Events and Information	Remarks and references to Appendices
BELGIUM BOIS D HAINE SHEET 6.	20.2.19		BATTALION SITUATED & EMPLOYED AS ABOVE. CASUALTIES - NIL.	
	21.2.19		DO. DO. 35 O.R.S PROCEEDED FOR DEMOBILIZATION. 2/LT H.C. DAVIES PROCEEDED AS CONDUCTING OFFICER. CASUALTIES:- NIL	
BRUSSELS SET "C"	22.2.19		BATTALION SITUATED AS ABOVE. HOLIDAY. 46 O.R.S PROCEEDED FOR DEMOBILIZATION. LT. E.S. BROWN & 2/LT J.M.S. BLAIR PROCEEDED AS CONDUCTING OFFICERS. CASUALTIES - NIL	X
HOO DOO	23.2.19		BATTALION SITUATED AS ABOVE. DIVINE SERVICES IN VILLAGE CHURCH 9 AM. CASUALTIES - 1 O.R. ACCIDENTALLY DROWNED IN CANAL AT LA CROYERE.	
	24.2.19		BATTALION SITUATED & EMPLOYED AS RANK. CASUALTIES - NIL	
	25.2.19		DO DO DO	
	26.2.19		DO DO DO No 300974 PTE. E. DEVENUP BURIED WITH FULL MILITARY HONOURS AT H.17.D.8.8. SHEET 46, COY 2. BELGIUM. -	
	27.2.19		BATTALION SITUATED & EMPLOYED AS ABOVE. 25 OR'S PROCEEDED FOR DEMOBILIZATION. LT N. MILLAR & 2/LT S. FOULDS PROCEEDED AS CONDUCTING OFFICERS. CASUALTIES - NIL	
	28.2.19		BATTALION SITUATED & EMPLOYED AS ABOVE. MAJOR. A DSO. M^cHARRIE. M.C. PROCESSED FOR DEMOB CASUALTIES - NIL	X

G. Marsh Lt. Col.
LIEUT. COL.
CMDG. 1/8TH ARG. & SUTHD HIGHRS

App 1 Roll of Officers
" 2 Fighting Strength.

1/6TH BN. ARG. & SUTHD. HIGHRS.

ROLL OF OFFICERS.

Rank	Initials	Name	Appointment
Lt.Col.	S.	COATS, D.S.O.	Brigade Headquarters.
Major	H.McC.	McHAFFIE, M.C.	Commanding Officer.
Capt.	J.A.	LATTA.	On leave.
Capt.	A.L.	PATERSON, M.C.	Div.Demobilization Officer.
A/Capt.	P.	HARRINGTON, M.C.	O.C. "C" Coy.
A/Capt.	A.	GARDINER.	Adjutant.
A/Capt.	R.W.	TURNER.	On leave.
Lieut.	J.H.	STOCKDALE.	Brigade H.Q.
Lieut.	G.B.	McGEE.	Hospital.
Lieut.	J.W.	MUNRO, M.C.	
Lieut.	A.	SHEARER.	Btn. Imprest Holder.
Lieut.	J.F.	ADAM.	1st Army Infantry School.
Lieut.	N.	MILLAR.	Conducting Officer U.K.
Lieut.	J.J.	CRAWFORD.	O.C. "A" Coy.
Lieut.	W.D.	BISSETT, V.C.	2nd-in-Command "C" Coy.
Lieut.	C.McC.B.	DUNCAN.	Conducting Officer U.K.
Lieut.	J.P.	CAIRNS.	
Lieut.	E.S.	BROWN.	Conducting Officer U.K.
2/Lieut.	S.	FOULDS.	do. do.
2/Lieut.	J.M.S.	BLAIR.	do. do.
2/Lieut.	R.S.	BROWNE.	
2/Lieut.	H.C.	DAVIES.	Conducting Officer U.K.
2/Lieut.	J.	HART.	O.C. "D" Coy.
2/Lieut.	J.B.V.	LINDSAY.	O.C. "B" Coy.
2/Lieut.	F.S.D.	STEPHENSON.	Conducting Officer U.K.
2/Lieut.	W.J.	YOUNIE.	do. do.
Capt.& Q.M.	J.	SCAIFE, D.C.M.	Quartermaster.

Attached.

Rank	Initials	Name	Appointment
Capt.	R.M.	FALKINER.	Medical Officer.
Capt.	J.H.	EDGAR.	Chaplain.

1/6TH BN. ARG. & SUTHD. HIGHRS.

FIGHTING STRENGTH.

REINFORCEMENTS.	O.	O.R.	WASTAGE.	O.	O.R.
Fighting Strength. 31/1/19.	42	888	Demobilized.	15	591
From Base.		9	C.C.S.	1	15
" 153rd Bde.H.Q.	1	1	Deserter.		1
" 153rd T.M.Bty.		6	Acc. drowned.		1
" C.C.S.		4			
" Corps Concent. Camp.	1				
TOTAL.	44.	908.	TOTAL.	16	608.
WASTAGE.	16.	608.			
TOTAL.	28	300.	28.2.19.		

WAR DIARY

1/6TH. BN. A. & S. H.

FOR THE MONTH OF

MARCH

1919.

Army Form C. 2118.

WAR DIARY
or
INTELLIGENCE SUMMARY.
(Erase heading not required.)

Volume XLVI.

1/10th Bn. Argyll & Sutherland Highlanders.

Place	Date	Hour	Summary of Events and Information	Remarks and references to Appendices
BOIS D'HAINE, BELGIUM. SHEET 6 BRUSSELS SET "C" 1/100,000	1.3.19		Battalion situated as per margin. Recreational Training. Capt. P. Harrington, M.C. assumed command of Bn. vice Major A.D.F.C. Inglese, M.C. demob. Lt. W.D. Bissett, V.C. assumed command of "C" Coy vice Capt. P. Harrington M.C. Capt. Revd. J.H. Edgar joined as Chaplain. Casualties - Nil.	
	2.3.19		Battalion situated as above. Divine Services in Village Church Hall.	
	3.3.19		Battalion situated as above. Recreational Training. Casualties - Nil	
	4.3.19		do do do Casualties - Nil	
	5.3.19		do do do	
	6.3.19		do do do Lt. G.B. McGee from Hos.	
	7.3.19		do do do Lt. G.B. McGee assumed command of "C" Coy	
	8.3.19		do do Holiday	
	9.3.19		do do Divine Services in Church Village Hall do	
	10.3.19		do do Recreational Training. 143 Other Ranks proceeded to Join 1/5th A.& S.H.	App. 1.
	11.3.19		Army of Occupation. Lt. W.D. Bissett, V.C. 2/Lt. J. Hart. 2/Lt. E.V. Lindsay. 2/Lt. R.S. Browne do. Casualties - Nil.	
	12.3.19		Battalion situated as above. Recreational Training. do	
	13.3.19		do do do Casualties - Nil	
	14.3.19		do do do 2/Lt. W.J. Younie from Leave do.	

WAR DIARY
or
INTELLIGENCE SUMMARY.
(Erase heading not required.)

Army Form C. 2118.

VOLUME XLVI.

Place	Date	Hour	Summary of Events and Information	Remarks and references to Appendices
SENEFFE BELGIUM SHEET 6 BRUSSELS SET "C" 1/100,000	15.3.19		BATTALION MOVED TO SENEFFE. ARRIVED NOON. 19 OTHER RANK PROCEEDED FOR DEMOB. CASUALTIES - NIL.	
	16.3.19		BATTALION SITUATED AS PER MARGIN. DIVINE SERVICES IN VILLAGE HALL & CHURCH. 2/LT. F.S.D. STEPHENSON FROM LEAVE.	
	17.3.19		BATTALION SITUATED AS ABOVE. 2/LT. H.C. DAVIES FROM LEAVE.	
	18.3.19		do. do. RECREATIONAL TRAINING.	
	19.3.19		2/LT. H.C. DAVIES TO U.K. FOR LEAVE & TO JOIN REGULAR BATTALION. LT. G.B. McGEE & 9 OTHER RANKS FOR DEMOB. BATTALION SITUATED AS ABOVE. HOLIDAY. CASUALTIES - NIL.	
	20.3.19		do. RECREATIONAL TRAINING. 2/LT. J.M.S. BLAIR FROM LEAVE.	
	21.3.19		do. do.	
	22.3.19		do. do. HOLIDAY.	
	23.3.19		do. DIVINE SERVICES IN CHURCH & VILLAGE HALL.	
	24.3.19		do. do. RECREATIONAL TRAINING.	
	25.3.19		do. do. do.	
	26.3.19		do. do. HOLIDAY	
	27.3.19		do. RECREATIONAL TRAINING. LT. A. SHEARER. LT. J.J. CRAWFORD. LT. C. McL. B. DUNCAN 2/LT. W.J. YOUNIE AND 9 OTHER RANKS FOR DEMOB. CASUALTIES - NIL.	

WAR DIARY
or
INTELLIGENCE SUMMARY.

(Erase heading not required.)

Army Form C. 2118.

VOLUME XLVI.

Instructions regarding War Diaries and Intelligence Summaries are contained in F. S. Regs., Part II. and the Staff Manual respectively. Title pages will be prepared in manuscript.

Place	Date	Hour	Summary of Events and Information	Remarks and references to Appendices
SENEFFE BELGIUM.	28.3.19		BATTALION SITUATED AS PER MARGIN. RECREATIONAL TRAINING. 2 OTHER RANKS FOR DEMOB. CASUALTIES - NIL.	
SHEET 6	29.3.19		do. AS ABOVE. HOLIDAY. do. do.	
BRUSSELS	30.3.19		do. DEVINE SERVICES IN CHURCH & VILLAGE HALL. do. do.	
SET "C"	31.3.19		do. RECREATIONAL TRAINING.	
1/100,000.				

APP. 1.	OPERATION ORDER.
APP. 2.	ROLL OF OFFICERS.
APP. 3.	FIGHTING STRENGTH.

Marshall CAPTAIN

OPERATION ORDER No.
1/6TH BN. ARG. & SUTHD. HIGHRS.

1. The train for personnel proceeding to 5th Argylls will leave MANAGE at 19.45 hours to-night.

2. Party will parade at Orderly Room at 18.30 hours.

3. Dress:- Marching Order with 2 blankets. Kilt aprons must be worn.

4. Transport Officer will arrange to collect valises of those Officers proceeding.
   2 "C" Coy.
   1 "B" Coy.
   1 "D" Coy.
   Valises will be ready by 17.30 hours.

5. Quartermaster will arrange to send 1 days rations from the reserve and 2 days rations will be drawn at MANAGE.

6. Lieut. W.D. Bissett, V.C. will be in charge of the draft. He will receive nominal roll, A.Fs.B.122 and kit deficiencies at the Orderly Room at 18.30 hours.

7. Personnel not proceeding will be concentrated near the Church this afternoon. C.S.Ms. will arrange direct with R.S.M. number of billets required.

8. All surplus blankets, stores, etc., will be sent to Quartermaster's Stores to-day. Coy. Commanders will certify that this has been done.

(Sgd.) A. Gardiner, Captain,
Adjutant, 1/6 th A. & S. Hrs.

10/3/19.

Copies to :-   Os.C. Coys.
               R.S.M.
               Transport Officer.
               Quartermaster.

App 1

1/6TH BATTALION ARG. & SUTHD. HIGHRS.

ROLL OF OFFICERS.

Rank	Initials	Surname	Assignment
Lt.Col.	S.	COATS, DSO.	Brigade Headquarters.
A/Capt.	P.	HARRINGTON, M.C.	Commanding Officer.
A/Capt.	A.	GARDINER.	Adjutant.
A/Capt.	R.W.	TURNER.	On leave.
Lieut.	J.H.	STOCKDALE.	Brigade H.Q.
Lieut.	J.W.	MUNRO, M.C.	Imprest Holder.
Lieut.	J.F.	ADAM.	1st Army Inf. School.
Lieut.	J.P.	CAIRNS.	Transport Officer.
Lieut.	E.S.	BROWN.	
2/Lieut.	S.	FOULDS.	Conducting Officer U.K.
2/Lieut.	J.M.S.	BLAIR.	
2/Lieut.	F.S.D.	STEPHENSON.	
Capt. & Q.M.	J.	SCAIFE, DCM.	Quartermaster.

Detached.

Rank	Initials	Surname	Assignment
Capt.	J.H.	EDGAR.	Chaplain.

1/6TH BN. ARG. & SUTHD. HIGHRS.

FIGHTING STRENGTH.

REINFORCEMENTS.			WASTAGE.		
	O.	O.R.		O.	O.R.
Fighting Strength, 31/3/19.	28	300	Demobilized.	10	64
From C.C.S.	—	7	51st Div. (H) H.Q.	1	—
" Base.	—	1	1/5th A. & S.H.	4	145
			C.C.S.	—	12
			Base, Etaples.	—	5
			Officers Club, Mons.	—	4
TOTAL.	28	308	TOTAL.	15	230
WASTAGE.	15	230			
TOTAL.	13	78			

App. 3

5 DIVISION. TROOPS.
1/6 (PIONEER) BATTALION
ARGYLL & SUTHERLAND
    HIGHLANDERS.
1916 JULY TO 1918 OCT
14 BN ROYAL WARWICKSHI[RE]
REGT (BECAME PIONEERS)
1918 OCT TO 1919 APR.

1538

www.ingramcontent.com/pod-product-compliance
Lightning Source LLC
Chambersburg PA
CBHW081442160426
43193CB00013B/2354